Testimonials

"The global Wikimedia community is constantly growing and changing, integrating new people and new cultures. FeverBee trainings and books have given multiple people on my staff deeper insight and fresh ideas for their ever-evolving roles in supporting them."

Maggie Dennis
Interim Chief of Engagement, Wikimedia Foundation

"Rich is a community-building veteran who consistently challenges the status quo, thinks critically, and drives results. His weekly newsletter is one of the few that I prioritize to read and learn from because it features real-life community case studies grounded in data and research."

Phoebe Venkat
Global Lead, Help and Engagement Communities, Facebook

"I've worked in the online community space for more than 20 years. When people ask my advice for the best resources to turn to about online community, I always point them to Richard Millington and FeverBee first. Richard's work is insightful, data driven, grounded in the reality of real organizational and workplace dynamics, and never loses sight of the big picture. If you're interested in building a great online community, Richard Millington and FeverBee is the single resource you can't do without."

Gordon Strause
Nextdoor / Director of Community

"FeverBee is essential reading for any community professional. Rich really spearheaded applying rigorous social science to the discipline of community management and holding the sector accountable to be better.

Liz Crampton
Community Program Manager, FitBit

"We have been following FeverBee since the early days of launching element14 and in this still new and evolving field, FeverBee has continued to be the voice of reason on all things community. Whether you are in the early days or working on a mature community, Richard provides the practical advice and constant reminders of things too important to overlook. "

Dianne Kibbey
Global Head of Community and Social Media, Premier Farnell\element14

"From the moment I started reading content from Rich I've always been impressed with his candor, willingness to challenge orthodoxy, and incredibly practical advice! And to this day he does not disappoint: I really like how he dispenses very useful advice and strategies, often backed by data and real-world experience. I've learned a lot from Rich!"

Cesar Castro
Sr. Director Adoption and Engagement, Salesforce

THE INDISPENSABLE COMMUNITY

Why Some Brand Communities Thrive When Others Perish

ISBN 978-1-947635-10-4 (Paperback Edition)
ISBN 978-1-947635-11-1 (Ebook Edition)

Printed in the United States of America
First Printing September 2018

Published by FeverBee

Contents

INTRODUCTION

On a cloudy San Francisco day in 2013, Allison Leahy, a novice with just a single year of community building experience, walked into 160 Spear Street to begin her first day of work. The offices felt busy, but rundown. Empty boxes littered the floors and were stacked high against the walls. Leahy's team consisted of just her and two colleagues. Within five years, they would build one of the most successful brand communities in the world.

Fitbit was six years old by the time Leahy arrived. The company was founded in 2007 by James Park and Eric Friedman, two computer scientists who realized the same accelerators used in the Nintendo Wii could be placed into smaller devices to track people's exercise. They scraped together $400k from friends and family and built a prototype tracker. They premiered at TechCrunch50, an industry startup competition, and came second. More importantly, they secured 2,000 pre-orders[1].

A year later, the pair released The Fitness Tracker, which could track footsteps, sleep and many other movements (or lack of them). Sales were slow at first. Fitbit sold just 5,000 by the end of the year. But it was enough to secure a big investment from a venture capitalist and a partnership with BestBuy. Sales rose rapidly from 58,000 in 2010 to 1.3m in 2012. The following year, Fitbit released their breakout product, the Fitbit Flex. Sales were heading into the stratosphere and the holiday season was only just beginning. This was a big problem.

A tsunami of new customers would soon flood Fitbit's tiny support team with questions. There was neither enough time nor money to train a new support team. But Fitbit already had over a million customers who had solved most problems.

---

1   https://www.wareable.com/Fitbit/youre-Fitbit-and-you-know-it-how-a-wooden-box-became-a-dollar-4-billion-company

Leahy's job was to build a community to connect the people with questions to the people with answers.

Leahy didn't have much time. She had to scale the community to handle the influx of members and get a lot more people answering questions. A new website was already in the works, but it needed to be tested and the community needed to support it. In early December 2013, Leahy invited 20 community members who had already answered a lot of questions (superusers), to join a customer council. Leahy hoped this group would not only test the new website, but also help answer a lot of questions over the Christmas rush[2].

Leahy and her team knew their customers were buying a Fitbit tracker to get (or stay) healthy. They would have questions about more than just the product: they would have questions about getting fit, eating well and having healthier lifestyles. The new community website wouldn't just be about Fitbit's products, but the role the product played in the lives of members. It would be a place for members to swap their best exercise, weight loss and healthy eating advice.

The new Fitbit website was launched just two weeks before Christmas. It had a tiny group of core users to answer questions, provided support in five languages and was designed to answer any product or fitness questions customers had. Now it was time to see if the community could handle an incredible influx of members.

The customer tsunami crashed upon the website hard over Christmas. On Christmas Day, 6,220 new members signed up with 1,254 posts (questions and answers). On Boxing Day, another 10,000 members joined and created another 2,000 posts, but the system held firm. Customers were asking and answering almost every single question. Even the healthy lifestyle area of the community was a hit. The tiny group of superusers Leahy recruited had helped her weather the storm.

By February, over 100,000 members had joined the community, yet the system was working. Members were stepping up and

2   https://community.Fitbit.com/council

answering each other's questions. Better yet, the superuser group had also answered the huge backlog of questions. Having shown the concept worked, Leahy was now eager to open the community up to the world.

So far, only registered customers could ask questions and see the discussions. This made the community exclusive, but more difficult to find. Anyone who searched on Google would never find the thousands of answers in the community. If Leahy could open up the community, its value would rise massively.

It took a year, but in July 2015, Leahy got the support she needed to let anyone browse the discussions in the community. The level of traffic rose by an incredible 500% in just six months. The significance of this is huge. If a customer asks a question of the community and gets an answer, they don't need to call customer support. But if that answer solves the problem for 500% more visitors, that's even more people who don't need to call customer support.

The community was now tackling all the questions it could see, but what about those it couldn't? Customers didn't just ask questions on the Fitbit website, they also asked them on Facebook, Twitter, and other platforms. If the community really wanted to show its worth, Leahy and her team needed to find a way to answer questions no matter where they were posted.

At that time, if members directed a question to @FitbitSupport, they would usually get a response. But if they casually mentioned Fitbit, their chances of getting an answer were slim. So, in summer of 2014, Leahy and her community team setup listening software to flag any mentions of the brand and respond to those they could help. They didn't just respond on Facebook and Twitter, they responded anywhere they could have an impact, including the forums of other brands. When QVC sold 62k Fitbit trackers, the support team answered questions in the QVC community too.

Most brand managers would be thrilled with a thriving community which answered tens of thousands of product-related questions every month. Leahy, however, wasn't satisfied; not yet. She had a bigger vision for the community: the community could be far more useful to Fitbit than just answering questions—it could help colleagues in other departments too. But to make this happen, she needed to build alliances throughout the organization.

In the Fitbit community, value comes from some unexpected places. For example, if the community management team knew what topics most people were talking about, they could tell the marketing team, who could create content they knew would be a hit. Even the most benign discussions now had great potential. One popular subject, debating whether a tuna or chicken sandwich was healthier, became an entire content series of 'quick lunch' ideas. Fitbit had nutritionists on staff who could quickly response to topics like these. Soon, all the best performing content was sourced from the community.

More alliances soon followed. The PR team began to use the community as an early warning system of problems and Leahy's team began responding to negative reviews on major shopping sites. Each alliance made Leahy's community more valuable to her colleagues. But, by far the most important alliance was with the engineering team. Engineering teams can now see how many times community members discuss a product issue and prioritize what to fix next. They get more insight into the customer experience and can find testers and gather feedback before and after every product launch. The community is now helping develop the very products they will soon be using. Today, Leahy feels the product feedback is even more valuable to Fitbit than the thousands of questions the community answers every week.

In the five years since first walking into work, Leahy and her colleagues have transformed a small, scrappy, community project into a core pillar of the business. At each stage they pushed the envelope of what was possible. They didn't wait for customers to come to them with questions, they went out to customers. They didn't hope people answered questions, they built a community council of top members to answer hundreds of questions each month. They didn't turn away members who just wanted to get fit, they created a place for them to have discussions about health and fitness.

Not everything has been a success. Leahy is quick to point out it helps to be working for a brand with a breakthrough product. And certainly no community can be a panacea for every problem a brand faces. The Fitbit community hasn't prevented a sales decline in recent years. But the overarching theme at Fitbit has been to continually drive the community to deliver the most value it possibly can to its customers and its members.

The community team today, which has grown to over 80 staff members around the world, now supports over 500,000 community members and several times more across social media. It delivers value to Fitbit's customers across the entire buying journey and even shapes the very products Fitbit releases. The community is a powerful testament to what a community manager with a big vision, great passion and indomitable determination can achieve. Leahy has done something far too few people building a brand community today even try to do: she's made her community *indispensable.*

Brand Communities Have To Show Impact

It's hard to find any major brand that hasn't tried to engage its customers online in some form, yet Leahy's success is surprisingly rare.

Most engagement efforts fail to gain traction while the rest fail to show results. Some struggle to even show a flicker of activity. Brands have even become increasingly keen to call their customers a community regardless if they've done anything to create one. As Fitbit's story shows, it's a waste of potential.

Indispensable communities—the kind both organizations and their members would struggle to live without—don't just appear through serendipitous luck. They are cultivated through a deliberate set of choices, a big vision, and a huge amount of persistence. They require a mental strength to not settle for an appearance of activity, but to push members to make *meaningful* contributions. They require a willingness to find out what colleagues need and design the community around those needs. They require a collaborative mindset, one that works with colleagues, not against them.

The nature of a brand community has completely changed in the past two decades. Until recently, any mention of a brand community would conjure up images of devout superfans of companies like Apple, Jeep, and Harley Davidson gathering together to celebrate their founder revealing a revolutionary new technology, help one another customize their vehicles, or participate in long journeys with one another. But brand communities now are completely different.

Today's brand communities are less about superfandom, creating warm, fuzzy feelings, and driving lots of *engagement* and instead more about showing a clear, impact. Making people feel great is nice, but being able to show millions of dollars in costs saved, new customers attracted, or new products launched as a result of the community is what matters. An upbeat, chatty, community that doesn't deliver any obvious results is a luxury few companies can afford (nor should they). It's not a ridiculous question to ask *"what's the purpose of all this activity?"* if the answer isn't readily apparently.

The work of building a brand community should be closer to what Leahy has done at Fitbit than what community professionals have done in the past. It's not only about responding to questions on social media or making customers happy, although both are important. It's about being specific in what the community offers the brand and always looking to expand that value. It's about finding out what members need and always looking to become more useful to members. It's about building alliances, a community of supporters throughout the organization.

Most importantly, it's about delivering the kind of value to both brands and members that only communities can offer. It's about being *indispensable*.

The Potential of A Community

The potential of brand communities today is bigger than it's ever been. Almost all brand communities have moved online and can reach far more people than they ever have before. They create resources and host discussions that millions read and watch. A dozen people might hear a useful tip shared over the barbecue at '*Camp Jeep.*'. Tens of thousands of people can read a Fitbit community post. Better yet, it can be tested, improved upon, and become *common knowledge* amongst all. It can drive forward innovation in ways that are scarcely imaginable.

Most community members will never meet one another, nor do they need to. They are less likely to be seeking a deep sense of belonging and more likely to be looking for something they need right now–expertise, a place to build their reputation, or a chance to help others and feel good about themselves.

With today's technology, and a generation that has grown up digital, there *should* be a lot more indispensable communities than there are today. Companies big and small are letting themselves and their members down. They lack the ambition for what a community could be and the determination to see it through. As the potential of brand communities has grown, the ambition of their creators has shrunk. It's a lot easier to launch another Twitter account than to take a group of customers aside and build something special.

Managing a community, and being responsible for a brand's best and most valuable customers, should be one of the most exciting and important jobs in any business. It should be a job others aspire towards and work to covet. But, too often, the task of engaging customers online falls to a junior staffer with limited experience. Too often, these staff are forced to chase meaningless measures of engagement rather than forging a powerful sense of community among their members and colleagues. It's impossible to build an indispensable community when we're forcing members to choose between clicking '*like*', '*share*', or '*comment*'.

The Indispensable Community

This book is about the brands that have built, nurtured, and developed *indispensable communities, the kind of communities that offer value impossible to capture anywhere else.* An indispensable community delivers results to multiple areas of the business.

Based upon interviews with over one hundred organizations and my company's work with over 250 organizations from around the globe, this book will help anyone managing a community to push back against the damaging quest for more engagement and pursue a more ambitious vision for community: to deliver the absolute best value for members and organizations.

Building an indispensable community comes down to answering three core questions:

1) What will motivate members to make their most valuable contributions?
2) How will we benefit from those contributions?
3) What is the sweet spot between what we need and what members want?

The book covers the process of turning members into allies, people who make their best possible contribution to a community with the time, talent, and motivation they have.

Then we discuss how to make the community indispensable to the companies we work for. It's about building internal alliances, overcoming resistance, and having a big impact upon many areas of the business.

Finally, the book shows you how to find that magic overlap between what a brand needs and what a member wants.

The Indispensable Community is more of a philosophy than a step-by-step roadmap. It's not simply a collection of tactics, although it does cover many of the most successful tactics. It's about having the right strategy and, more importantly, the right mindset for a community to become indispensable.

The goal of this book is to ensure brands aren't creating *just another community*, but are instead working to build a community that is indispensable to themselves and their members.

PART 1
TURNING MEMBERS INTO ALLIES

Chapter 1

WHAT DO MEMBERS WANT?

In late 2007, Anthony Goldbloom, an econometrician for the Australian Treasury, won a coveted 3-month internship with *The Economist* in London. He spent the first two-and-a-half months writing about the exploding financial crisis. Then, in his last few weeks, he pitched a piece about a topic that was close to his heart: *predictive modelling*.

Predictive modelling uses past data to build models to predict future outcomes. For example, a bank might use past customer data to predict the risk of future customers defaulting on a loan and use this data to decide whether to grant the loan (and at what interest rate).

Goldboom soon discovered one of the great advantages of writing for *The Economist:* he could secure interviews with almost any chief information officer (CIO) on the planet. Goldbloom was stunned to learn most CIOs shared the exact same problems. They struggled to find qualified staff and predict customer acquisition and retention rates. These were the very problems Goldboom already had the skills to solve. The only thing he lacked was the qualifications:

> *"I knew I could code, I knew statistics, but I had no real way to prove I could do that job and solve their problems."*

Never short of ambition, Goldbloom soon came up with what he describes as a *"meritocratic labour market"*. Essentially, this is a place where people can prove how good they are without official qualifications. His vision was simple. If data professionals had access to the same datasets and were set the same task, it would be possible to assess the abilities of each without any official qualifications.

By 2010, this idea had become Kaggle, a community for data professionals. Kaggle began life as a competition site. A company could post a sample of a dataset to the community and teams of data scientists would compete to build a model that predicted the next numbers in the set. At the end of the competition, the company revealed the rest of the data and whichever model yielded the closest results won. The winning team received a prize and the company got a model they could use.

The challenge was finding a good enough data set to get started. Until he proved the idea, few organizations wanted to share their data. Goldbloom needed something that would both capture people's attention and had enough existing data for his audience to play with. He found his answer in a singing competition.

The Eurovision Song Contest has been running since the mid-1950s. Each participating European country nominates an entrant[3]. After each entrant has performed live on TV, the population of each participating country votes for their favorite act. These votes are counted by country and each country distributes their points using a positional voting system (i.e. the top act gets 12 points, the next act gets 10, and the following acts receive 8 to 1 points each)[4]. Whichever act gets the most votes, wins.

In theory, the best performance should receive the most points. In practice, countries tended to exchange points with their nearest neighbors. For example, Greece traded points with Cyprus, The Netherlands traded points with Belgium, and the Baltic states had a tendency to vote for each other too. This might not be great for a fair singing competition, but it's perfect for Kaggle's first competition. It allowed people to use historical voting patterns to make predictions.

Goldbloom announced the competition on every stats blog, newsletter, and user group for data professionals he could find. A total of 22 teams signed up and submitted their predictions. The BBC even cajoled their top data scientist to submit an

---

3   In recent years non-European countries such as Australia have been
     allowed to compete.
4   Countries can't vote on their own acts.

entry[5]. It was time for Goldbloom to put his vision for a merito-cratic labour market to the test. Could uncertified amateurs match qualified professionals? In the days prior to the competition, Goldbloom published Kaggle's consensus prediction and compared it with the betting markets[6]. Then he waited for the show to begin.

As the confetti cleared, Goldbloom emerged victorious. The Kaggle consensus predicted seven of the top ten results. The betting markets predicted just five. Kaggle's winner wasn't the BBC's top statistician, but an amateur named Jure Zbontar[7]. The amateurs had resoundingly defeated the professionals.

Next, Kaggle's members were invited to predict which patients would respond to HIV treatment. If the Eurovision song contest results built Kaggle's reputation, the HIV treatment competition brought the potential of Goldbloom's model into sharp focus.

In total, 107 teams entered the competition with a promised prize of $500 (plus an opportunity to co-author a paper with Goldbloom). The top 15 teams outperformed the best methods in academia. Once again amateurs crushed the certified pros. The winner, Chris Raimondi, was an English major drop-out who taught himself machine learning from free YouTube videos. He beat the team behind IBM Watson to accurately predict changes in viral loads with a 77% accuracy, compared with just 70% for the best methods in scientific literature. Goldbloom's meritocratic labour market was alive and kicking.

More competitions followed and with similar results. Kaggle soon introduced a ranking system. Every member on Kaggle is ranked from 1 to 1.2m (as of Sept, 2017). These rankings place members within one of six levels. Around 0.15% are *grand-masters*, 1.4% are *masters*, 4% are *experts*, and the rest are novices and contributors. According to Goldbloom, the world's top tech companies will gobble up anyone at the master and grandmaster

---

5   http://news.bbc.co.uk/1/hi/programmes/more_or_less/8697176.stm

6   http://blog.kaggle.com/2010/05/25/
     eurovision-predictions-statisticians-pick-azerbaijan/

7   http://blog.kaggle.com/2010/06/09/computer-scientist-jure-zbontars-
     method-for-winning-the-eurovision-challenge

level. A headline for a *Wired* article about Kaggle agrees: "*Solve these tough data problems and watch the job offers role in.*"[8]

Kaggle's top ranked member, Gilberto Titericz Junior, was an electric engineer in Brazil in 2012. Now, like almost every top member, he's working for a top tech company in Silicon Valley. The most elite job adverts for data scientists today even include winning Kaggle competitions as a requirement.

However, competition sites are typically cursed by success. As competitions grow more popular, the odds of winning plummet, and fewer people participate. But this wasn't happening at Kaggle. The site was becoming more popular with each competition. As Goldbloom explains, he soon realized it wasn't competitions people wanted, it was the datasets used for the competitions:

> "*The biggest problem data scientists have is getting access to high-quality data sets. If you can give them interesting data sets, they will do interesting things with them.*"

This led to a new area solely for members to share great datasets, an area that fast became more popular than competitions. Kaggle became known as a place where members could get great data sets to practice, test, and advance their skills.

As the community grew rapidly, members also wanted a better place to chat with each other outside of competitions. In 2011, Kaggle launched a forum. Interestingly, members began to use this forum not just to chat but also to share their code and analysis. They were looking for somewhere to share this information and the forum provided it.

So Kaggle launched a new dedicated area of the site named Scripts (later rebranded as Kernels). Kernels, Goldbloom explains, are essentially a *workbench* for data scientists and statisticians. They are a place for members to store, share, and work on their scripts. Over time, Kernels became the most popular area of the site, with competitions dropping to what

---

8   https://www.wired.com/story/
      solve-these-tough-data-problems-and-watch-job-offers-roll-in/

Goldbloom estimates was around 15% of the total level of activity. This changed Kaggle's mission too. It moved away from competitions and towards what Goldbloom describes as "a place where data scientists do all of their work."

Since Kaggle's launch, Goldbloom has been remarkably effective in tracking what his members need and delivering on those needs. Kaggle was never designed as a place for people to chat - there were plenty of communities for that; it's a place to solve important problems. Kaggle has gradually become an *indispensable community* for its members.

Data scientists need Kaggle to get access to great datasets and know which cutting edge tools the world's best are using to win competitions. They need Kaggle to store their work, collaborate with others, and get feedback from the best in the world. They need Kaggle to build their reputation and gain access to the best jobs in the world. Kaggle is the kind of community that does what communities should do, *improve the lives of people it touches.* It wasn't a surprise when Google acquired Kaggle in March 2017.

Too few communities become as indispensable to its members as Kaggle. Most brands are creating communities. This creates a ferocious war for attention. Many respond to this competition by making it easier to participate, asking their members for less, and hoping they can build a community around whatever activity they get. Kaggle proves it doesn't work that way.

The secret isn't to ask members for less, but to ask members for more. It's to get members making their best possible contribution to the community. It's to get members making meaningful contributions to worthwhile projects. It's mostly about knowing what members want and turning them into ALLIES.

Turn Your Members Into ALLIES

The best communities get their members to *Advocate, Lead, Learn, provide Insights, Educate* others, and *Support* the community. In practice this means:

1) **Advocate.** Members promote the organization and its community to others. Members provide referrals, share

content, provide testimonials, and create reviews. This brings in new members and, more importantly, new customers.

2) **Lead.** Members organize and lead groups within the community. These groups help prevent information overload, keep members hooked, organize contributions, and ensure the community achieves its maximum potential.

3) **Learn.** Members learn something that matters– new skills, solutions to their problems, the latest news, trends, or social norms. When members read discussions, articles, attend webinars, and much more, they learn. Learning reduces support costs, improves satisfaction, and often generates new business.

4) **Insights.** Members directly or indirectly help to improve products by making suggestions and highlighting problems, providing qualitative and quantitative data via habits which can be mined for useful insights. Often members don't even realize they're doing this.

5) **Educate and Support.** Members contribute to the collective good of the community. They share their best tips, answer questions, share links, and support one another. Often they take volunteer roles to keep the community on track.

The contributions to the community listed above will be remembered for months, even years, from now. Naturally, it's an awful lot easier saying this in theory than getting members to make these contributions...and, most importantly, *to keep making these contributions.*

What Motivates Community Members?

Wouldn't building a community be a lot easier if we knew what our members wanted? If they carried around signs clearly telling us what they needed?

Academics have spent the past 30 years tying themselves into knots trying to explain why people participate in online communities. Do members carefully consider whether the rewards (information) exceed the costs (effort) and then decide whether to contribute? Are people just naturally drawn to be a part of social groups and join the brand communities for which they have the most affinity? Or is it about website design and technology? Perhaps it's just a habit? If we believe the academics, the answer is '*yes*'.

In 2012, FeverBee tried to incorporate most of these ideas into a single model, which has served us well over the years. The model recognizes not all visitors are highly motivated and what brings people to a community usually isn't what keeps them there. Time and time again, we've seen this model predict what gets people to participate in a community.

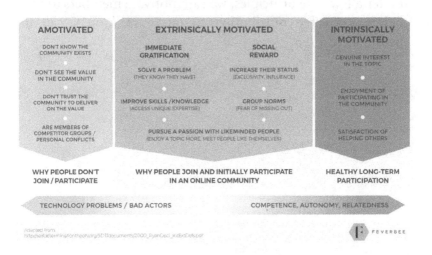

The first column is easy. Members won't visit a community unless they know it exists, can see the value, and trust it will deliver on that value. But even when they do, they still won't visit without some sort of trigger. If they have a product problem, want to get better at what they do, or suddenly find themselves wanting to connect others, they will visit the community most likely to help.

The problem is, most people visit a community once, find the answer to their problem, and leave, never to return. This is where motivational factors come in: competence, feeling a sense of progress and getting better at the topic, autonomy, feeling free to pursue an interest in the topic, and relatedness (or relationships) with others. These kinds of motivation make the topic more interesting, the community more fun, and give members a sense of satisfaction from helping others. But this won't happen if the technology is tricky, or trolls and spammers overwhelm the site. The technology needs to be kept simple and the spammers need to be kept in check.

So how do we get members to make the best contributions they possibly can and overcome the barriers which might prevent them from participating? In chapter after chapter, with brand after brand, we'll see the same principles at work. Every community is unique, every member is different, but if we master a few core principles, we can motivate members to make their best possible contributions to the community. We can turn them into ALLIES.

Chapter 2
ADVOCACY

After two years' of research, Frederick Reichheld, Director Emeritus at Bain & Company, published an article in 2003 that changed how companies think about customer satisfaction[9].

Before Reichheld, it was hard to measure customer satisfaction. Most customer satisfaction questionnaires were filled with a complex set of questions each referencing a different attribute of the product. Customers rarely bothered to complete them and data analysts struggled to extract useful insights from them.

Reichheld compressed the entire problem into a single question: *How likely is it that you would recommend [your company] to a friend or colleague?*. Survey participants were asked to rate their response on a scale of 0 to 10, where 0 is not likely at all and 10 is very likely. Reichheld divided these responses into three categories. Those who score 0 to 6 are 'detractors', 7 and 8 are 'neutrals', and 9 and 10 are 'promoters'. The detractors are then subtracted from the promoters to reveal a single all-encompassing score, the Net Promoter Score (NPS).

The NPS score is widely used to measure customer satisfaction and predict growth. It's also used for brand communities. CMX, a community hub, did a survey that revealed 25% of people managing communities today use the NPS score to measure their success[10].

But the NPS score has its criticisms too[11]. Do promoters actually do much promoting? Do the same people who classify themselves as eager to promote the brand actually do it?

---

9   https://hbr.org/2003/12/the-one-number-you-need-to-grow
10   https://cmxhub.com/community-value-metrics-research
11   https://www.van-haaften.nl/images/documents/pdf/Measuring%20 customer%20satisfaction%20and%20loyalty.pdf

DocuSign And QuickBase

By late 2015, Jonas Tichenor, DocuSign's new Director of PR, was ready to admit the advocacy effort had been a miserable failure. The community, which had launched in 2012, was supposed to build an army of advocates eagerly promoting the company across the web. However, at its peak, it had just 15 actively engaged members. This was a devastating result after three years of work[12].

Survey after survey showed DocuSign had thousands of so-called promoters, according to NPS scores[13]. Although they seemed willing to do it, they just weren't promoting. Tichenor and his team suspected two explanations. First, community members weren't asked to do anything useful:

> "We were basically saying to advocates, here is an advocacy community platform, just go do whatever you want," Tichenor admitted.

And what they wanted, it seemed, was to chat about random topics. An audit of discussions showed 70% of activity in the advocacy community was off-topic, whimsical, discussions. One of the most popular was: "What's your favorite holiday sweater?"

The second problem was DocuSign wasn't being proactive enough. The very people who had said they were willing to recommend the company weren't being asked to join the advocacy community.

The first step, as Tichenor's colleague Laura Olson explains, was to get serious about the community. This wasn't a place for people to chat about holiday sweaters or what they had for breakfast. Members needed to spread the word and get rewards:

> "We focused community activities on things that mattered. We asked advocates to share their useful stories for the sales team, publish their successful case studies, provide testimonials and recruit their friends."

Asking members to do something that mattered had immediate results. It brought in new sales leads, created new content for

---

12   http://videos.advocamp.com/watch/fBwsR1Rs3v8758cMuZpVRf
13   DocuSign classifies anyone who scores an '8' as a new promoter.

marketing material, and provided the sales team with fantastic stories to use in their pitches. DocuSign rewarded these advocates in a variety of ways. Some of these perks were intangible, like the opportunity to beta-test new products, others were more concrete, like receiving company sweaters or riding in a limousine during the DocuSign's annual customer conference.

Once Tichenor and Olson had actively engaged the small number of existing members in the community, they invited their promoters to join. According to Tichenor, this astronomically increased the number of advocates. Over 3,000 new invites were sent by community members to new prospects in a single year.

The pair then built profiles of top advocates and began browsing the DocuSign university, the existing customer support community, and other channels, looking for people who matched the profiles. Those whom matched the profiles were invited to join the community.

The results were phenomenal. Within a year, these new advocates had completed 12,500 acts of advocacy and generated over 300 leads for the sales team. This helped Tichenor gain the budget to hire staff and invest more in growing the advocacy community. But the benefits didn't end there; as Tichenor explains, advocates also began helping each other to advocate:

"They began asking and answering advocacy questions. One advocate posted a question asking for a 60-second elevator pitch to help the CTO understand why they needed to expand usage of the product. This generated 35 responses within 2 days."

This elevator pitch response was especially notable. Not only did it secure a far bigger purchase from one client, but it also provided the answer for many other customers to explain the benefits of the product to their boss and senior executives.

In the years since, Tichenor has found increasingly sophisti-cated ways in which advocates can help promote DocuSign:

"We want them to share quotes, blog posts, speak at our events and third-party events. We have great advocates who just upon the ask would show up on the [sales] phone call or go to our event and speak to hundreds of people about our journey."

The lesson from DocuSign's advocacy community is having a lot of *promoters* is great, but they're not going to do much promoting without some sort of trigger. And the best trigger is the brand finding exciting ways for members to advocate.

Across the country, in Cambridge, Massachusetts, Intuit's Davin Wilfrid was learning a similar lesson at QuickBase[14]. QuickBase is a platform that allows non-technical people to develop apps without having to code. By 2015, QuickBase had 58,000 customers and super high NPS scores but, as Wilfrid notes with disappointment, less than 20 reviews on the key platform comparison sites.

QuickBase's promoters weren't doing much promoting and those who did weren't doing it well. The reviews often used incorrect language or failed to stress the key points QuickBase needed to make. Some even placed QuickBase in the wrong category or supplied old and outdated information.

In the world of business software, reviews on comparison sites are king. Before making a big purchase decision, buyers want to know what others think. By Wilfrid's reckoning, almost all business software sales begin with an online search and over half of these land on a review site. This makes reviews an asset worth cultivating.

Wilfrid had studied his customer's buying journey and decided to focus on getting members to leave reviews on three key review sites he felt would have the biggest impact. But unlike DocuSign's Tichenor and Olson, Wilfrid couldn't just ask his community members to post more reviews if the reviews themselves weren't great. He needed good reviews that clearly highlighted what made QuickBase unique and different. He needed to educate his customers:

> *"We had a conference where we completely surrounded our best customers with all the right messages,"* says Wilfrid. *"This also came through in webinars, surveys, and any other touchpoints we had with advocates."*

---

14   http://videos.advocamp.com/watch/LHxUEAPvv8rUu-MqkCx44Q

After the conference was over, Wilfrid asked his members to leave a review on a single website, G2Crowd. Within days, QuickBase doubled their number of reviews and had become the top-rated software company in the right category. Equally important, *they were using the right terminology.* According to Wilfrid, this really helped gain internal support:

> *"Our leadership team freaked out when they we showed them people were leaving reviews, using our language - we're number one in this category."*

QuickBase now had over 120 reviews on G2Crowd alone.[15] These reviews not only persuaded prospects to sign up but they helped other departments too. The marketing department got the exact text and messaging to use as part of their social strategies. The product team got to see what they should fix next. The sales team got hundreds of great third-party reviews they could send to prospects. Most importantly, advocates got an incredible feeling of knowing they had made a difference.

None of this would have happened if Wilfrid hadn't asked his members to promote the company and trained them how to do it well. Advocacy needs a direct approach. There is no shame in asking members to promote a brand if those members are happy to do it. Once they are willing to do it, then QuickBase's success shows it helps to identify where in the buying journey advocates can have the biggest possible impact and help them to have that impact.

The best advocacy programs never passively wait for members to help out. They tell their members what they need and give them all the resources and support to help them be the best advocates they can be. In return, they get members who create promotional content on social channels, share news and discounts, write positive reviews and testimonials, publish case studies, speak at industry events, and directly tell their friends to buy from the brand. Most importantly, their members *enjoy*

---

15   https://www.g2crowd.com/products/quick-base/reviews

doing these things. They enjoy the perks and they enjoy feeling like they matter. It's a win-win.

Hewlett-Packard

Advocacy is the single easiest way to get better results from the community, yet very few communities are doing it. Part of the problem is not knowing where to start. Not every member is destined to become a great advocate. It's easier to pick people who have already rated themselves as likely to promote the brand and give them something to do. But getting started without this data is trickier.

When Chris Peltz and his colleagues were launching HP's first ever advocacy program, they began with people who were already advocating. They dug up people who had already written reviews, responded to comments on social media, and shared HP content. From this group, Peltz found 111 members before the community had even launched.[16]

Next, Peltz began seeking recommendations from his colleagues, especially those who were in close, frequent contact with customers. This included customer success teams, product management, and those running customer advisory boards.[17] Finally, he looked at who was speaking about the products at events, attending webinars, sharing advice in online forums, and responding positively to customer support surveys.

In less than nine months, Peltz had built a community of just under 1,000 members participating in hundreds of acts of advocacy each month. Obviously, it's a lot easier to build an advocacy program when you start with people who already advocate. The most successful advocacy programs begin with the members most likely to advocate for the organization and gradually expand the circle from there. But finding advocates is only half the battle; keeping them is harder.

---

16   http://videos.advocamp.com/watch/ynbfLzINPb7GeG8f4w8JYw
17   ITSM - IT Services Management Community.

Influitive

Mark Organ, the CEO of Influitive, a customer advocacy platform, believes the secret to keeping advocates lies in the interplay between what he describes as micro-factors (immediate rewards) and macro-factors (broader sense of purpose and meaning).

Influitive, for example, is one of several platforms that lets members collect points and exchange them for prizes. Customers can earn dozens of points by completing a simple task such as leaving a comment on a blog post and thousands of points by generating qualified referrals or bringing in new business. Any brand can easily set powerful prizes for members who earn a vast number of points (e.g. an all expenses paid trip to your the company's factory for those that reach 500,000 points).

Points for prizes are clearly micro-factors. They're the immediate rewards for completing a task. They are the instant gratification people want right now. However, as Organ clarifies, these micro-factors wear out after a period of time. There needs to be a bigger reason why advocates are there. This is where Organ believes macro-factors come into play.

Macro-factors are a sense of tribal identity, believing in the group's mission, knowing that contributions have an impact, and helping members achieve their goals. According to Organ, while members may join for initial rewards, in the process of feeling more in control over the outcome, more able to pursue what they most enjoy, and more socially connected to others, they become intrinsically motivated. This leads to a genuine interest in the topic and enjoyment of helping others.

Long-term advocates are much less interested in points than feeling closer to the organization, feeling a sense of community, and seeing the impact of their contributions. The *community* aspect of advocacy is critical here. By seeing other advocates doing the same thing, celebrating each other's successes, getting to know one another, members can feel this sense of being a part of something bigger than themselves. They can see and benchmark their own contributions against one another.

It's not essential to launch a new community platform to make this work; any brand can invite a group of customers to join any online group platform and reward members for completing tasks. Over time, they will build a sense of community between them. It's this sense of community that keeps members coming back.

Summary

Advocacy is the most valuable thing any community member can do, yet too few are being asked to do it today. What's the point of building a happy, satisfied, community if members aren't doing anything that helps?

Finding great advocates shouldn't be a difficult challenge. Almost all brands have some advocates: people who are already writing great reviews, talking about them on social media, and sending in their feedback. It's easy to begin small with a group of community members and give them tasks.

These assignments need careful consideration. For some it might be direct referrals, for others it will be reviews. Sometimes it's simply useful to have a few customers who can hop on a sales call with a prospect and share their experiences. There is no shortage of ways a customer can advocate for a brand they want to help. The challenge is to identify what offers the highest impact and give them all the resources and support they need to do it.

But advocates want something in return. At first, that's likely to be an immediate reward, perhaps unique points or access to key staff members. Sometimes it's something more distinctive, such as a limousine ride to the company conference. But all tangible perks fade over time. Once again, members want to matter. They want to get benefits from participating in the community, which only the community can provide. These are deeper emotional benefits than tangible rewards. They want to feel they had a big impact, want to feel a part of the organization, and want to feel a sense of community with one another.

Chapter 3

LEADING

For the past 15 years, thousands of gamers have fought for control of the galaxy. This war peaked in 2014 when 717 corporations (teams), from 55 alliances, formed two coalitions for the largest battle in digital history: The Bloodbath of B-R5RB.

In 21 hours, 7,500 gamers fought for control of a star system. Thousands of ships, with a real world value of $300,000,[18] were destroyed. By the end of the battle, The Clusterfuck Coalition and Russian Alliances had seized control of the star system.[19]

CCP Games launched EVE Online, a massive multiplayer online role playing game (MMORPG), in 2003, and it's been running ever since. CCP Games takes a notoriously laissez-faire approach to managing their community. Some players want to mine and trade resources in distant solar systems, others want to form alliances, betray their brethren, and do whatever it takes to get ahead. With few exceptions, anything goes. Since its launch, plenty of games with better graphics, gameplay, and support have come and gone, but EVE Online still survives. It's not the game that keeps people coming back, it's the community.

Lone rangers don't last long on EVE Online. To get the most from the game, a player needs to join a team (known as a corporation). Each corporation is led by a CEO (team leader). These CEOs are almost entirely independent from CCP Games, yet CCP Games relies on them to keep players paying their $15 subscription fee. As PC Gamer magazine explains:

"[...] players in EVE Online have to make their own fun. It's a burden carried by the leaders of these thousand-player

---

18   Calculated by converting EVE Online money to current exchange rates.
19   https://www.wired.com/2014/02/eve-online-battle-of-b-r/

alliances to continually keep their pilots entertained with new wars, fights, and reasons to play each day."[20]

The game's CEOs have almost presidential powers. They can tax their members, set economic policies, and coordinate ambushes against unsuspecting players. For security and support, corporations often work together to form alliances. Alliances issue press releases, solicit investments for future projects (using game money), and join with other alliances to form huge coalitions when a big battle is brewing.

Paul Elsey, a former avid player, now CCP's community manager, explains how leaders even build their own communication systems outside of CCP's control: "*Some individual alliances have their own sub-communities within the game. These guys host their own forums, voice comms servers and have their own infrastructure using tools like Hipchat (private text chat) and Discord (voice chat).*"

The sparsely populated realm of a digital galaxy is an unlikely place to draw lessons for people building brand communities today. But it highlights critical human behavior–*most activities are a lot more fun in the company of others.* Not just any others, but smaller groups where members can build friendships and feel they have an impact. It's a lot harder to feel connected to a mass of online strangers than to a handful of people we've seen around often and repeatedly interacted with.

Past a certain level of activity, the interests and needs of members diverge too much to imagine it as just a single group. Instead the community needs sub-groups. These subgroups can drive incredible levels of growth, amazing contributions to group projects, and bring in a lot of advertising revenue. But every sub-group needs something too many consider as an afterthought. Sub-groups need leaders.

Leaders have their own needs and motivations. Sometimes they go rogue and do irreparable harm. Sometimes they get started, lose interest, and leave empty shells behind that linger

---

20   https://www.pcgamer.com/
       why-eve-onlines-million-dollar-battle-was-a-huge-bust/

in the community. Others are enthusiastic but don't direct their energy to anything useful.

This chapter is about the organizations who have made leadership work, who have nurtured leaders, ensured they create the right kind of groups, and stopped them from going rogue. Most importantly, it's about the different models of nurturing leaders, from EVE Online's *laissez-faire* model through tightly controlled models.

The Community Lifecycle

By the time Alicia Iriberri, a research assistant and Ph.D. candidate, and Gondy Leroy, an associate professor at Claremont Graduate University, published their masterpiece[21], academics had already been studying virtual communities for almost 30 years. To say they hadn't achieved much, would be mean - they had published a huge number of studies - but the result was a jumbled mess of competing and conflicting ideas about how communities grow. Each felt communities could be explained through their discipline (computer science, sociology, management, psychology, information system, etc).

Iriberri and Leroy, instead of trying to prove which discipline was right, showed how each subject was useful but at different stages of the community lifecycle. Their lifecycle (adapted by FeverBee below) had different stages. Communities needed different things at each stage to progress to the next.

Iriberri and Leroy noted that to progress beyond maturity and have a sustainable community, there needed to be sub-groups. As communities get busier, information overload becomes a big problem. It becomes more difficult to feel a sense of intimacy with other members and so the needs and interests of members begin to diverge. Unless the community forms sub-groups, members drift away until only a core-group remains. This is borne out by data. Communities without sub-groups tend

---

21 A. Iriberri and G. Leroy, "A Life Cycle Perspective on Online Community Success", *ACM Computing Surveys*, 41 (2), Article 11, 2009. doi: 10.1145/1459352.1459356

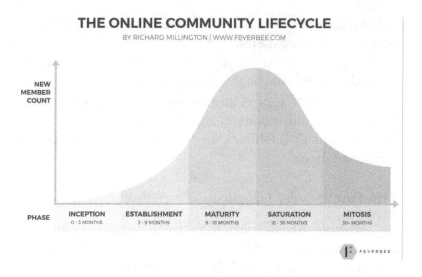

THE ONLINE COMMUNITY LIFECYCLE
BY RICHARD MILLINGTON | WWW.FEVERBEE.COM

PHASE	INCEPTION	ESTABLISHMENT	MATURITY	SATURATION	MITOSIS
	0 - 3 MONTHS	3 - 9 MONTHS	9 - 18 MONTHS	18 - 36 MONTHS	36+ MONTHS

NEW MEMBER COUNT

FEVERBEE

to have a tiny group of active members and a large group of members who have drifted away. Without sub-groups, a community is just a mass of strangers lobbing content at each other, hoping to gain a fleeting amount of attention. Sub-groups make a community better.

But letting members create their own own sub-groups has well-documented problems. If the community is just getting started, too many sub-groups diffuses the activity over too many places. It's usually best to start with one group and expand over time. A bigger problem is empty shells. Once members find they can create their own sub-groups, many decide to do it. They soon realize it's hard work and give up. Yet these empty shells linger on, ruining the experience for everyone on the platform.

Organizations have tackled these problems in three distinct ways. These can be classified as *no control, some control,* and *full-control. No control* is when the organization plays, at best, a supporting role. It provides the technology and resources but usually stays out of the way and lets leaders lead. *Some control* is when the number of groups is restricted or members have to pass certain criteria to run them. It usually also means the leaders can be removed if they're doing a bad job. *Full control* is when the number of groups and the leaders running them is decided by the organization. As we'll see, each of these approaches has its advantages and disadvantages.

Wikipedia

On the morning of March 11, 2017, 132 Wikipedians entered the Museum of Modern Art in New York to participate in the world's biggest editing marathon. By 5pm, they had added a combined 27,400 words, via 789 edits, across 168 articles to Wikipedia. These numbers might not seem like much, but this was just 1 of *175 events* taking place around the world as part of Art+Feminism's annual Wikipedia edit-a-thon[22].

Art+Feminism is on a mission to increase representation of female artists and address Wikipedia's gaping editorial gender imbalance. That March, 2,500 participants from 37 different chapters around the globe created 2,000 new entries for female artists and improved 1,500 articles.

Art+Feminism is one of thousands of member-led initiatives around the world committed to improving Wikipedia. Other popular projects include *Wiki Loves Monuments*, a global photo competition in which 10k+ photographers compete to take the most impressive photos of buildings of major cultural significance; *Wiki Loves Earth*, which focuses on images of the planet; and *Wikidata*, which encourages people to share data easily read by machines.

These member-led projects contribute thousands of articles, provide an incredible collection of royalty-free images, and useful data support for Wikipedia. *Wiki Loves Monuments* is recognized by the Guiness Book of Records as the largest photography competition on the planet.[23] More importantly, it serves as a terrific recruiting tool for new editors. It's a lot easier to become an editor when in the company of other editors.

---

22 http://www.artandfeminism.org/
23 http://www.guinnessworldrecords.com/world-records/
    largest-photography-competition/

Most impressively, The Wikimedia Foundation (the charitable trust that owns Wikipedia), doesn't create these projects, it doesn't organize these projects, and it doesn't provide on-site staff to support them. Everything is organized by passionate, motivated leaders. But the Wikimedia Foundation does provide leaders with one resource they really want–money–to ensure the foundation's most passionate supporters are contributing towards goals.

Sure, anyone can come up with a project, get a group of friends together, and start making entries without any financial support at all. But the most committed volunteers can apply for grants to support their vision. Almost 30% of The Wikimedia Foundation's annual budget is set aside as grants for their leaders. Each year, the foundation sets goals and provides funding to members who come up with projects. The grants can't be used to replace volunteers (i.e. leaders can't pay themselves or others). They're mostly used to cover expenses for events, travel, and some software. It's a remarkably simple but effective model. Almost any brand can copy it. It doesn't take much to identify the community's priorities and set aside a few thousand dollars for leaders who want to create a sub-group to achieve them.

If EVE Online represents the most extreme version of *no control*, the Wikimedia Foundation retains only slightly more control. The foundation lets anyone lead but only supports those who have a reasonable shot of achieving the organization's goals. The Wikimedia Foundation tries to make informed guesses about which leaders will have the biggest impact and gives them the support they need to achieve it. This approach limits empty shells but can also lead to waste if the leaders don't reach their goals. A more common (and potentially more effective) approach is being pioneered by Facebook today.

Facebook

In early 2018, Facebook's CEO and founder, Mark Zuckerberg, unveiled a noble new corporate mission: *"give people the power to build community and bring the world closer together. That reflects that we can't do this ourselves...."*[24]

Facebook had always enabled leaders to step forward and lead as many groups as they liked. Once a group was created, leaders were usually left alone with little interference–or support–from Facebook. However, the change of mission changed the approach to leaders. Now, Facebook would begin proactively *supporting* leaders.

This support comes in three forms. First, Facebook invites leaders with 10k+ members to exclusive 'power admin' groups. This provides a private place for group admins to get emotional support, share advice, and stay in touch with the latest tools and tactics at their disposal. Second, Facebook drives more traffic to popular Facebook groups. Popular groups are more likely to be suggested to friends. This helps groups gain the traction they need to thrive. Third, Facebook hosts frequent in-person Community Summits to bring together the best of the best. This is a great way to build close relationships with top group admins and learn their needs. These relationships, as we will learn later, might also prove critical to preventing rebellions.

Unlike the Wikimedia Foundation, Facebook isn't trying to guess which leaders succeed. Facebook picks from those who are succeeding, letting natural selection work its magic. Some groups thrive, others perish. Facebook works with the thrivers. This approach is a lot easier to manage and focuses Facebook's efforts on those with the best track record of success. It's an easy, low-cost way to make groups work.

The downside of this approach is that it leaves behind a long trail of empty shells. Most groups have failed, but Facebook doesn't replace bad group leaders or shut down dead groups. This both hurts members' likelihood of joining future groups and doesn't look great. Another problem, as Reddit has discovered, is leaders who have created their own groups

---

24   www.facebook.com/notes/mark-zuckerberg/
      bringing-the-world-closer-together/10154944663901634/

without much support have a worrying tendency to go rogue when they dislike something the brand does.

Reddit

On June 10, 2015, Reddit's new CEO, Ellen Pao, introduced a policy that should have generated considerable applause but instead forced her resignation.

Pao announced Reddit would remove five 'subreddits' (separate groups run by 'moderators') filled with hate-speech. This included the infamous 'r/fatpeoplehate', a subreddit with 150,000 subscribers dedicated almost entirely to mocking photos of the obese.

Prior to Pao's appointment, Reddit had tolerated many controversial subreddits under a policy that favoured freedom of expression. Leaders of subreddits had been given free reign to run their fiefdoms as they pleased with little inference from Reddit. While this created a remarkable diversity of subreddits, it also let a tiny number of subreddits cause remarkable harm to Reddit's reputation, a reputation increasingly associated with the small minority of subreddits dedicated to hate and abuse.

The backlash against Pao's announcement from leaders of many subreddits was swift and acute.[25] Some subreddit leaders asked their members to sign a petition calling for her resignation. On July 2, 2015, a staff member responsible for running the popular '*ask me anything*' (AMA) series was fired by Reddit (although not by Pao). In response, leaders of popular subreddits launched '*AMAgeddon*' and suspended their subreddits in protest. Pao resigned a week later.

Pao's story illustrates the tricky balancing act of letting leaders lead. It's hard to attract and keep great, passionate leaders without providing them the freedom and ownership to do as they choose. However, the more freedom they have, the more

---

25 Many subreddit leaders supported the ban, but had concerns about enforcement of the ban.

harm they can do. As Reddit has learned, it's very difficult to recover from a negative perception.

The Reddit model is similar to Facebook. Almost anyone can create and run a subreddit. The best groups rise to the top. But there are two main differences: a) failing leaders can be replaced and b) subreddits comprises basically the whole of Reddit. Without subreddits, Reddit doesn't exist. This gives leaders far more influence at Reddit than they have at Facebook. They have the power to go rogue when they're unhappy.

But is there a solution to stop leaders going rogue? Are rogue leaders an inevitable price to pay for allowing anyone to run sub-groups in the first place? Or are there lessons to learn from organizations who have gotten this right?

According to Evan Hamilton, Reddit's Community Team Leader, the blackout (AMAgeddon) was a cry for help from passionate moderators who didn't feel they were being listened to or had the tools they needed.

Part of the problem was simply a lack of resources. At the time, Reddit had just 60 employees, whereas sites of similar size had thousands. In August 2017, Reddit announced they had received $200m in additional funding[26] and quickly expanded the company to over 280 employees. This coincided with a huge internal push to support the community team. Today, the community team is the biggest it's ever been and has the bandwidth to focus specifically on community engagement. Hamilton explains this has allowed the community team to vastly improve the communication between moderators and Reddit:

"We now provide several subreddits devoted to moderator[s] [...] I'm trying to push the team more into education and engagement. So over the past year, we've been doing these Friday fun threads in the mod support channel, just engaging with the mods in an instance when they don't have an issue, because when you only talk to someone when you have an issue, you don't build a very deep relationship."

26   www.recode.net/2017/7/31/16037126/
      Reddit-funding-200-million-valuation-steve-huffman-alexis-ohanian

This push towards deeper engagement has reduced ticket response times to moderator questions and resulted in 100% of moderator questions receiving a response.

Reddit also went on the road. During 2017, Reddit staff hosted events in six cities across the USA to thank moderators and learn more from them. Between 40 to 100 people turned out for each, a tiny fraction of the 148,000 Reddit moderators, but Hamilton points out these discussions had a real impact on both Reddit staff and moderators:

> *"Our community team has a good relationship with the mods, but [for] the rest of the company, it's not part of their job day-to-day to interact with them. So we brought people from every department in the company, especially from the Product team because they build things that directly affect mods."* Hamilton continues: *"We literally had product launches come out of those conversations because what moderators do is so unique and specialized that you [may] understand the general idea, but once you actually have a conversation you realize, 'Oh, this is what your day-to-day experience is like. How can I help you with that?'"*

Reddit has also worked hard to develop a reasonable appeals process for moderators who feel unfairly treated and do everything possible to educate and assist moderators before taking any action to enforce their policy. If a subreddit is sitting empty and someone else wants to run it, they can put themselves forward to do so.

Since implementing the changes, Reddit has seen fewer bad headlines and an increase in subreddits. According to one study, *"More [user] accounts than expected discontinued using the site; those that stayed drastically decreased their hate speech usage—by at least 80%."*[27]

There isn't a silver bullet solution to keeping great leaders on your side, but investing heavily in direct communication certainly helps. Hamilton and his team engage in constant, never-ending efforts to build stronger relationships with leaders,

---

27   http://comp.social.gatech.edu/papers/cscw18-chand-hate.pdf

through multiple channels, and constantly make improvements. Reddit might get to set the rules, but they need the trust of leaders if they're going to be followed. To quote Henry Kissinger: *order cannot simply be ordained; to be enduring, it must be accepted as just.*

Reddit, Facebook, and Wikimedia represent the three most common approaches to nurturing sub-groups. Each enables (almost) anyone to create a group, but supports them in different ways. Wikimedia Foundation picks and helps those most likely to succeed, Reddit and Facebook support those who are succeeding. The Reddit story highlights the danger in giving leaders too much power. The more influence leaders have, the more resources Reddit has to spend keeping them onsite and constantly engaged. A less common, but potentially more effective, approach is to be more cautious about who can create and run groups.

Mozilla

Mozilla is more dependent upon volunteer leaders than almost any other organization. It is an open-source community best known for developing the Firefox web browser[28]. The core source code is developed and maintained by passionate volunteers from the community, which makes the community quite literally indispensable.

Any developer can download Firefox code, find something they want to improve, and suggest a change. These changes are reviewed by other volunteers who, as in any peer review system, might accept the change, ask for further changes, or reject the addition. If accepted, it then goes through a process known as '*automated testing*', after which it is in incorporated into the next update.

However, as the community grew, it became impossible to keep using the same management methods. The diversity of

---

28   Open source essentially means the code is open for anyone to use and adapt to their needs. You can download the code and edit it for your needs.

volunteers, the types of contributions volunteers could make, and the ambitions of the organization made it impossible. As Mozilla's Rubén Martín explains, it wasn't viable to keep providing the same level of support via support staff:

> "We used to have community managers on the ground working with people in different regions around the world providing one-to-one help. But this wasn't really scalable over time. It was really difficult to support everyone."

So Martín created Mozilla Reps, a program to support around 200 volunteer leaders who want to become official representatives of the organization in their region. Mozilla provides their reps with resources, training, and support to organize events, recruit and support new contributors, and document activities.

To Martín, Mozilla Reps not only solves the scalability issue but it also aims to be the bridge between Mozilla and its communities:

> "When Mozilla is launching an initiative, we know most people representing our local communities. We deeply involve the reps council in strategic conversations and get their feedback. They highlight local needs which we incorporate into our objectives. Once we establish our priorities, it's the reps who mobilize local groups, universities, and others to be involved."

Mozilla Reps has been around in various forms since 2011, but it's only recently been given a mandate to shape how the rest of the organization deals with volunteers. Today, reps get the same level of access to Mozilla's internal systems as any employee. They can access internal meetings, documents, and any other resources. They can also be nominated for the reps council. This council is responsible for managing a budget and distributing funds and swag. A volunteer can approach the council with an idea, present a case, and receive funding from the council.

However, this means bad reps also have the ability to cause chaos. Rubén and his team therefore need to be cautious in who they allow to run groups and the rewards they offer them.

Today, anyone who has been a volunteer for a year can apply to be a rep. A group of volunteers reviews the process of recruiting and onboarding reps.

Reps are expected to be enthusiastic about Mozilla's mission and willing to go through Mozilla's onboarding process. This includes training in Mozilla's values, diversity and inclusion, and community participation guidelines. The onboarding program provides a framework and a specific set of tools to help Mozillians to organize and/or attend events, recruit and mentor new contributors, document and share activities, and support their local communities better.

Mozilla doesn't reward reps with money, and opportunities for recognition are limited. The main benefit of being a rep is having direct access to Mozilla and the ability to have a noticeable impact towards Mozilla's mission. Mozilla Reps aims to find people passionate about its mission and provide them with all the support and training they need to mobilize their local community to make a difference.

The program has driven some remarkable results. In 2017, reps organized over 1,000 events, tested 6,250 websites, and contributed more than 25k sentences in a wide range of languages to support Common Voice, an initiative to help teach machines how real people speak.

The Mozilla model is one in which Mozilla creates leadership roles and invites members to apply for them. This keeps the power largely on Mozilla's side. Leaders who don't abide by the rules can be replaced by those who will. However, Mozilla also provides members with a remarkable level of access and control over their fiefdoms. This satisfies the motivations of members. It's not an easy balance, but it's delivered great results for Mozilla.

StackExchange And Preventing Bad Leaders

Joel Spolsky has a simpler approach to preventing bad, negligent, and lazy leaders: *don't let them run groups in the first place.*

Spolsky is a co-founder of StackExchange, a network of 170+ communities built and managed by passionate leaders. Where most communities are designed for free-flowing discussions supporting multiple opinions, StackExchange's mission is to find and show the single best, member-created answer to any question.

StackExchange began as StackOverflow, a single site for programmers, in 2008. Prior to StackOverflow, communities for programmers were terrible. People with questionable expertise were giving bad and grammatically incorrect advice. The best answer to a question was as likely to appear on the fifth as on the first page of responses.

StackOverflow overcame this problem by combining a typical online forum experience with modern innovations. Members could vote on the best answers, edit and update previous responses and reputation systems to highlight the smartest members. The community exploded to life and Spolsky soon decided to licence this technology to anyone who wanted to create their own site.

The idea bombed. Very few people were able to grow their communities to a critical mass of activity. It wasn't a problem of technology, it was a problem of leadership. Few people had both the time and talent to manage a community. Joel and his co-founder decided to make two major changes.

First, they made the site free for everyone to create their own community. StackExchange would own and monetize the sites through advertising. However, this alone would have risked the same problem: *a lot of empty groups founded by leaders who don't have the time, talent, or motivation to manage them over the long-term.*

To overcome this problem, Spolsky and his team created *Area51.* While StackExchange claims Area51 is an incubator for new sites, it's better imagined as a gladiatorial gauntlet designed to weed out all but the most committed of leaders. In Area51, anyone can propose an idea for a new site, but the odds on any site making it through to launch is slim.

The process begins by creating a proposal on the site. This alone requires a reputation score of at least 50, earned through previous contributions to the network. Once the proposal has been submitted, members progress to the *definition phase*. In this phase, group creators need at least five example questions and five users willing to follow the proposal within three days to avoid being deleted.

If the proposal meets this criteria, it then has 90 days to attract 60 followers, 40 questions, and 10 votes. These votes help define what the site will be about. If the proposal survives the moderator chopper (many ideas are also merged or rejected for being too similar to existing sites at this stage), it moves into the *commitment phase*.

In the commitment phase, group creators need to earn a 100% commitment score. This means at least 200 committed members, 100 of whom need to have a reputation score of 200+. A commitment isn't made lightly; it's an obligation to ask or answer 10 questions in the private beta phase. A member can only commit to one project at a time and a commitment means a member is putting their own reputation on the line to help someone else. If they fail to follow through (as many do), their reputation score drops. For StackExchange members, whose reputation score often helps them with future job applications, this is a big deal.

Yet, in an evil twist, the value of a commitment fades over time. If the proposed community doesn't get enough commitments fast enough, it might need more than 200 committed members.

Once a proposed community has achieved *a 100% commitment score*, its site enters a 90-day *private beta* phase. In this phase, only those who committed to the site are allowed to participate. The group creator can can now seed the site with questions, create an FAQ, and bring some moderators aboard. This phase checks the site has legs to grow and flourish. It also checks some basic assumptions. For example, did those who committed to the site actually participate? Did the discussions take off and develop? Are the discussions broad enough? Do enough expert members from other StackExchange sites participate in this private beta?

Even after reaching this stage, it's still possible the community will be scrapped if it doesn't get approval from the community team. For example, below is a post from Robert Cartaino, StackExchange's Director of Community, on a startup community in the private beta phase:

> *"[...] we also have some grave concerns about the scope and direction this site has taken. The vast majority of questions seem to be very narrowly focused on the mechanics of STARTING a business rather than the meatier challenges of actually running a start-up. There's nothing inherently wrong with a few how-to-get-started questions, but right now the front page reads more like any chapter-book on "How to Start Your Small Business" rather than something that captures the insightful day-to-day problem-solving of actually running a small enterprise."*

If the private beta is successful after 90 days, the site enters a public beta phase. This is where anyone can join and participate in the community. The purpose at this stage is to get the creator to evangelize the community and get more people to join. The site remains in public beta until it attracts an average of:

- 10 questions per day.
- 90% answered questions
- 150 users with a 200+ rep.
- 10 users with a 2000+ rep
- 5 users with a 3000+ rep
- 2.5 answers per question.
- 1,500 visits per day.

Public sites can languish in this phase for years without becoming part of the StackExchange network (at the time of writing, the Board and Card Games Stack Exchange site has been in a public beta for almost *7 years*).

If the community makes it past this stage, it's finally added to the StackExchange network for all to see and join. Area51 might be brutal, but it prevents the network becoming filled with ghost towns. Only the very best and most committed leaders are left standing. The results speak for themselves. By 2015, StackExchange had 170+ different sites each led by dedicated (volunteer) leaders. These sites attracted 3.9 billion visits from 5 million registered members in a single year. Today, it's ranked among the top 120 websites in the world.

Summary

Communities only reach their potential when they unleash the passion and talent of their leaders to build their own groups. These groups make the community better. They help members find their tribes, drive great collective contributions, and prevent information overload. Once the community becomes too big to follow, subgroups are essential to keep members hooked.

However, not all leaders are equal. Some are well-intentioned and eager to help. They will naturally do a good job and rise to the top. Others are negligent, lazy, and prone to outright rebellion if they have a grievance. The last thing any organization wants is the very leaders they've nurtured to turn against them or leave thousands of dead groups in their disinterested wake.

The five models covered above (and shown below) show several options to tackle this. There are many different ways to motivate and influence leaders. They range from EVE Online's 'anything goes' to StackExchange's 'iron grip' approach. Each has its pros and cons.

	Who can lead?	Level of support	No. of groups	Pros	Cons
Anything goes (EVE Online)	Anyone	Tech only	Unlimited	Leaders have full control. Low cost.	No control over leaders who can harm the brand by association.
Pick the winners (Wikimedia Foundation)	Anyone	Financial	Unlimited	Biggest impact for resources. Medium cost.	Can waste resources if they fail.

	Who can lead?	Level of support	No. of groups	Pros	Cons
Support the best (Facebook)	Anyone	Best groups get promotion and expertise.	Unlimited	Supports people who prove they can succeed. Medium cost.	Great leaders might slip through the cracks.
Support the interested (Reddit)	Members with a 50+ Reddit score.	Tech/social	Unlimited	Supports people who want to maintain a good relationship.	Doesn't focus on those who can have biggest impact. High cost.
Create roles (Mozilla)	Need to apply.	Training program / full access.	200	Retains power. Medium cost.	Limits potential no. leaders.
Iron grip (StackExchange)	Prove they can lead a group.	Promotion on very popular site.	One group per topic.	Retail power and keeps only the best leaders.	Deters many great leaders. Very high cost.

Ultimately, the more control any organization tries to exert over their eager leaders, whether that's limiting who can become leaders or what those leaders can do, the more they have to offer. Sometimes, simple name recognition is enough. Being associated with running a group on a wildly popular site is a big reward in itself. Sometimes it's unique access and taking on a rare role, something any leader can take pride in. Other times it's direct communication and financial support.

Each model is different, but everyone building a community does need to decide which model is best suited to them. How will we support leaders and ensure we're getting the most from them?

Chapter 4

LEARNING

Imagine a world where no customer would be kept on hold for endless minutes by customer support and every possible question received an answer within seconds, not hours. Timo Tolonen, GiffGaff's Head of Community, and his team have been trying to create such a world. Tolonen claims his community answers questions posted in the community in an average of 90 seconds.

Although it's a bold claim, we can easily test it. At 15:21 on the 29th November, 2016, I posted a question in the community.[29] By 15:23, two people had replied, one with a detailed five-paragraph answer. That's a staggeringly quick response.

GiffGaff was founded in November 2009 as a 'SIM-only' telephone operator. Soon after, the customer community was winning awards for its trailblazing approach to customer support[30]. GiffGaff doesn't have a frontline customer support service, and offers no number to call for help (the irony isn't completely lost on a mobile phone operator). As Tolonen explains, all but the most sensitive of requests are handled by dedicated members of the community. Customers can ask a question in the community and have a response in 90 seconds.

This has yielded incredible financial benefits for GiffGaff. In the last nine years, customers have asked just under a million questions. If we assume the average cost per customer call in the UK is £3.50 ($4.70), it means, if just half the questions in the community are answered (and we estimate it's a lot higher), the community has saved GiffGaff at least £1.75m ($2.34m).

---

29   https://community.giffgaff.com/t5/Help-Support/
     Business-account-going-from-3G-to-4g/m-p/19651586#M6998280
30   http://blogs.forrester.com/groundswell/

Without the community, GiffGaff would've been forced to hire a legion of staff to provide 24/7 support. Today, it has almost no customer support staff.

But this back-of-the-napkin calculation grossly underestimates the real value of a support community, which doesn't come from people who ask questions, but people who look for an answer in search engines. These are two very different groups.

At GiffGaff, the titles of search results show whether the problem was solved or not. Members who click on the answer will immediately see the question and can click on 'go to the best answer'. GiffGaff shows the reputation score of the person who provides the best solution. This lets visitors decide if they trust the solution. Within 30 seconds of searching for a solution, most visitors will have the answer without even needing to ask the question.

Customer support centers are inherently wasteful. Most customer support representatives repeatedly solve the same few problems—the same problems most customers already have overcome. Some companies try to get around this by creating *frequently asked questions*, but there are only so many questions that can squeeze into an FAQ (and most customers ignore them anyway).

A far more efficient approach is to have a huge community database of questions. Ideally, these questions have been asked in many different ways, so customers are more likely to find their solution. Each solution can then be read by hundreds, even thousands, of people. This isn't an exaggeration. While GiffGaff doesn't show how many people visit a post, plenty of other communities do and the numbers are staggering. For example, a single post taken at random from the customer support community at Dropbox (a file hosting service) has been viewed over a thousand times[31]. That's up to a thousand people who didn't need to call customer support because they got their answer from someone else's question.

---

31   www.dropboxforum.com/t5/Installation-and-desktop-app/
      Folders-on-external-hard-drive/m-p/223819#M44431

These people have earned a rather unfortunate name: *lurkers*—those who visit and browse, but don't participate. Yet lurkers are the most valuable asset most brand communities have simply because there are usually far more lurkers than participants.

Customer support agents don't distinguish between a call or ticket from a lurker or active participant. One either picks up the phone or writes an email; their problems cost the same to resolve. A community certainly needs active members to participate, create questions, and answer them, but the real value to GiffGaff isn't the relative handful of members who participate, it's the *thousands who get their answer without having to participate.*

Almost every public community is packed with lurkers. For every person who participates, up to a hundred more might be quietly lurking. The GiffGaff community shows a few dozen questions asked in the last hour, but, for example, 2,614 registered members could be online with another 3,149 guests browsing. This means just a few dozen people are participating, but 5k+ people are watching. These 5k people are getting their answers without having to participate. Once lurkers are included in the value of the community, we can start to see the real value of a brand community.

If we consider the tens, hundreds, or even thousands of people who get their answers without having to ask a question, we can start to multiply our earlier figure (£1.75m) by the number of visitors, often 10x or 100x more, to see the community's true value (£10.75m, £100.75m etc...).

However, as Tolonen explains, *"it isn't just a cost-saving exercise, it's a better way of providing service."* He had the data to back him up. In 2017, Which? (the UK's most popular consumer association),[32] polled 4,000+ customers from 14 different telephone operators across the UK. GiffGaff ranked first for customer service, with an 81% positive rating (a remarkable feat in an industry where bad customer service is the norm).

---

32   Which? is also a FeverBee client.

The GiffGaff community isn't just providing cheaper customer support, it's providing *better* customer support.

This chapter is about lurkers (better deemed   learners). It's about how brands like GiffGaff, Apple, and BestBuy have designed their communities to help members learn solutions to problems, supply great tips and advice, the latest trends, and more. Most brand communities are badly designed. They're leaving thousands, if not millions, of dollars on the table by not harnessing the true value of the people who will never participate, whose names they will never know, whose data they will never capture.

Because we can't see learners, it's easy to ignore them, to assume they're perfectly happy doing what they're doing and can be left alone. It's easy, instead, to design the entire community around the needs of the tiny number of people who do contribute. But it's a mistake.

We've seen just how valuable lurkers can be when a community is designed for them. Just as advocates can be better advocates, and leaders can be better leaders, so too can learners be even better learners. They can learn more than they do today. They can learn the very best advice from the very top members. But only if the community is designed for them.

It's tempting to try to turn learners into participants. They can be urged to sign up, share content, or ask a question. While it might tempt a few, it usually does more harm than good. It gets in the way of what learners came to the community to do, *learn.*

Even if learners were afflicted by a sudden, overwhelming, desire to participate, most wouldn't have any pressing questions to ask or new expertise to share. No matter what a brand does, most of its audience will never participate. But they don't need to participate to be incredibly valuable. Instead of turning learners into participants, it's a lot more effective to make sure they're learning well. In short, if people are going to lurk, turn them into the best possible lurkers they can be.

If a visitor only has time to read three to five articles per week, which three to five articles will they see when they visit the community? If they're looking to solve a problem, how can we reduce the time it takes to show them the solution? If they want new tips, how do we help them identify the best tips?

Members can learn far more from a community with the right design. They can harness the real value they get from the lurkers. Incredible, endless, opportunities exist to design a community that can deliver a lot more value to learners and a lot more value to the brand. This chapter shows how to design a community to ensure learners are getting the most possible value.

HackerNews

No one calls a customer support line to catch up with their favorite customer support rep. Most people only visit customer support communities when they have a problem—maybe once a week, once a month, or *never*. They usually don't have enough problems to make the support community a regular habit[33].

Every brand is also capable of designing a community to go beyond just support, a place where people can solve a broader number of problems and get tips to improve their lives. One of the best examples of this is HackerNews.

By late 2006, YCombinator, a startup accelerator, had funded just under 100 startups and was finding communication between founders increasingly difficult.

A startup accelerator helps promising companies grow their business. In exchange for approximately 7% of their profit, YCombinator provides seed funding, advice, and connections to help members grow. A critical part of their support is helping founders learn everything they need to know to excel, from staff, previous program graduates, and from one another. As YCombinator grew, it faced the challenge of disseminating the best ideas and advice between members without flooding

---

33   Worth noting: if members do have a lot of questions, that isn't exactly a good sign; it means a lot of members have problems with your products or services.

everyone's emails. As YCombinator's co-founder, Paul Graham, explained in 2007:

> *"We've now funded about a hundred people, so it doesn't work well anymore to send links around by email."*

Graham decided to tackle this problem by creating a new community to share the best startup related news, links, and advice.[34] Startup News was launched on February 19, 2007, and became an instant hit. Part of the community's success was drawing technology professionals who missed the early days of Reddit:

> *"We wanted to try to recreate the way Reddit felt back in 2006, when the users were mainly hackers," Graham says. "As Reddit became more popular, its focus inevitably changed. This was good for most users, but it left some of the earlier ones feeling left out. We wanted to create a new home for people like us."[35]*

Startup News (rebranded as HackerNews) functions a lot like Reddit. Members can share and vote on interesting stories. The most popular stories naturally rise to the front page. As the community grew, making the Hacker News front page became a badge of honour, which could drive tens of thousands of visitors to the company[36].

What makes sites like HackerNews so powerful is their addictive nature. It's addictive in the same way email is addictive. Every time you visit, you might find something new and exciting. As Graham described two years after launch:

> *"I'm all too aware how addictive HackerNews can be. For me, as for many users, it's a kind of virtual town square. When I want to take a break from working, I walk into the square,*

---

34   Paul Graham also wanted to use the community as a proof-of-concept of Arc, a programming language he had developed.
35   https://news.ycombinator.com/hackernews.html
36   https://ryanwaggoner.com/
      the-secret-to-hitting-the-hacker-news-front-page-and-what-its-worth/

just as I might into Harvard Square or University Avenue in the physical world.[37]"

HackerNews has a different psychological relationship with members than GiffGaff. Rather than a community to solve problems, it's a community to share new information. Some information is entertaining, some is provocative, and some is just really useful advice. Members visit to see what's new or what peers are doing (a bit like Facebook, but with a greater focus on sharing good links).

HackerNews provides a venue for hundreds of thousands of programmers and startup founders to learn what's new, what's popular, and get the best ideas in the technology space at any given time. But social news sites, like HackerNews, aren't the only option to keep members visiting every day. Many ways to design a community for members to learn or get something new on every visit are possible.

For example, Figure 1 is an app that, on every visit, shows members photos of new and interesting medical cases. A new case pops up immediately when they open the app. Other examples of communities include social networks that include a mixture of personal updates and news, and sites like Quora, Medium, and others, which show members new posts on every visit.

GiffGaff, HackerNews, and Figure1 show members what they're looking for. They teach, demonstrate solutions, communicate news and offer interesting and relevant stories. This only represents a tiny sliver of what members can learn from the community. Members can learn a lot more when they're shown information they're *not* looking for.

What Do Members Learn In A Community?

Every time we walk into work, meet with friends, or hang out in a WhatsApp group, we're learning a lot more than we realize. Sure, we're learning what's new in people's lives, we might ask their help on a personal problem or their opinions on the

---

37   http://www.paulgraham.com/hackernews.html

latest political scandal. This is all explicit information sharing: information we're looking for and information our buddies are happy to give. But this is just the tip of the iceberg. We're picking up cues on how others behave, how they dress, how they speak. We're learning the information we didn't know we didn't know. We're learning what Donald Rumsfeld infamously termed the *"unknown unknowns."*[38]

When a community starts giving members information they weren't looking for, it becomes a lot more valuable. Members are often learning things from members (sharers) who are unaware they are sharing useful information. We can see this in the table below:

		Learners	
		Know they don't know (information they're looking for)	**Don't know they don't know** (information they're not looking for)
Posters	**Know they're sharing**	Answers to problems Tips and Ideas Reviews and experiences	News
	Don't know they're sharing	Trends	Social norms

Almost every community naturally focuses on giving members the information they know they want, whether it's solutions to a problem (GiffGaff), new tips and ideas (HackerNews), or reviews and experiences (TripAdvisor). Almost all the web traffic to a community comes from people looking for this information.

But then the competence, autonomy, and relatedness factors creep in. Members want to feel smart and part of the group. This usually means also learning news from peers, the latest trends, and social norms. The best communities, deliberately or not, surprise members with information they didn't even know they needed. A great example of this is news and gossip.

For example, below is a conversation hosted in Sephora's BeautyTalk community:

---

38   https://www.youtube.com/watch?v=GiPe1OiKQuk

1:56am - 1tinybubble - *"Heads up for those who are thinking of the Sephora Fav - ultimate travel bag. It has a "only a few left" message on the US site."*

2:08am - 1tinybubble - *"seems like they restocked a few previous sephora favs but no Soko set in sight."*

08:19am - Astray - *"It's showing online but OOS [sic].....has anyone bought it or is it just sitting there waiting to go live? I soooooooooooo want this today! Haha!"*

08:51am - Shayog - *"It is possible that Sephora is putting a few of these kits up for sale every couple of hours. It is also possible considering the amount of people who are waiting for this kit for it to sell out instantly, especially if people are buying more than one at a time.*

01:26pm - Shayog - *"It's live!!!!"*

01:30pm - makeuplovertay - *"Ladies & gents, as of 3:29 pn CST - all items were available, in stock and ready to buy! GO GO GO"*

01:45pm - mella900 - *"got 2 sets of soko to tokyo. my FOMO has been relieved"*

01:45pm - KarinaGG - *"Has it been up for Canadians?"*

01:51pm - Niki172 - *"yay got mine!" :)*

02:37pm - Astray - *"YAY! It's live! Thank you Sephora!"*[39]

None of these members were visiting the community to see if the bag was sold out, or when it would next be on sale, but the news quickly spread. It's information members loved but never knew they wanted. One way to help members learn more from the community is to show the latest news (or gossip) from members.

Then there is also information members might seek out, but people who have it don't realize they're sharing it. Kaggle's CEO, Anthony Goldbloom, touched upon this:

"Kaggle has become a place to go and stay up to date with what's happening in data science. Our competitions, even if

---

39   https://community.sephora.com/t5/Beauty-Confidential/
Sephora-Favorites-Sets-share-your-thoughts-questions-and-pics/m-
p/2492226#M98310

you don't participate, are a good way to keep up with learning [sic]. When we started in 2010, most winners used Random Forest. Today this has been superseded by Gradium boosting and deep neural networks"

For the non-data scientists amongst us, Goldbloom is saying the community is a place to ensure members are using the same tools as the very best in their field. This kind of information can be built into the community. Member profiles can feature what products and software members use (with regular surveys/ summaries), a common practice in gaming communities where members often post their setup in their profiles. It's a trend others pick up on and begins to spread. Every member in every community is drawing conclusions from the tools and activities of other members. Finally, information learners aren't aware they need and sharers aren't aware they're sharing are the social norms, the behaviors members consciously (or subconsciously) pick up on from one another as they spread among the group. If everyone in our peer group is wearing a hat, odds are we will too. It's a way of signalling we're a part of the group.

The difference between a social norm and a trend is subtle, but worth mentioning. A trend is what a growing number of people are doing. A social norm is what the majority of members (or those considered peers) already are doing. Some communities make it easy to see what's popular within the group, to encourage more of this behavior. Bodybuilding.com, for example, spreads the norm of sharing before and after photos. Members know to regularly update each other on their progress.

As Sephora no doubt knows, if a social norm benefits the brand, the brand wins. Members sharing photos and stories of themselves using the the product spreads a powerful social norm. The entire discussion on Sephora (mentioned above) took place within a broader discussion titled *'Sephora Favorites Sets: share your thoughts, questions, and pics'*. This was a 1,300+ post discussion featuring members sharing their photos of favorite Sephora products. It's not hard to see the social norm established here.

Members are learning far more from a community than we imagine. We can deliberately design communities to pick up on the latest trends, social norms, and more. This makes the community even more valuable to our members and to the brand. It can even create a brand that becomes the focal point for the entire sector. This can only work if the community is designed to give members the right information.

The Most Valuable Thing Members Can Learn

Most communities are badly designed. This doesn't mean they're not easy on the eye—some are beautiful monuments to great taste—but they aren't designed to help members learn what they are supposed to learn.

At the top of almost every online brand community website sits a banner. If we imagine a community as Manhattan, the banner is Times Square. It's the most valuable real estate in any community. It's a single, decisive opportunity to deliver your most relevant message. It's a unique chance to show exactly what the community is about, who it's for, and what information members will get. It's exactly where brands should *not* put a bland message inviting people to *connect, share, and get involved.* Which, sadly, is what most brands do.

What members see when they visit a community for the first time shapes their relationship to the community. If, for example, they see the latest problems solved, they will visit when they have a problem they want solved. If they see the latest tips, they will visit when they want useful tips (more often). If they see the latest trends, most popular members, or social norms, it will be a place they visit to keep updated on what's happening (they will visit *a lot* more often).

This isn't an afterthought – it's the entire ball game. Whatever the goal of the community is (e.g. customer support, keeping customers, innovation, etc.), members have to see the right information to match.

Going From 0 to Millions of Members

When Ed Giansante took over the reigns of the Dropbox community in 2014, the level of activity (40 to 50 news posts each day) was manageable. It was easy to respond personally to each post or find a small group of top members to help out. But as the community grew to 300+ posts per day, this approach didn't works.

The same frequent questions were getting many different answers, making it difficult for learners to know which was the best solution. Worse yet, more and more members searching on Google were landing on older, outdated, information. The simple system that worked well when the community was small was failing as it grew.

A good analogy is a disorganized bookshelf. When there are a few dozen books on the shelf, it only takes a minute or two to scan through and find the right title. But when a few thousand books are on the shelf, you need some sort of system—and it has to be the right system. Imagine if libraries displayed books by the date they received them or by which were most popular.

In Facebook's early days, members could see every action their friends took on their wall. However, as members became more connected, games were launched, and brands joined the fray, it soon became impossible to follow this much activity. Much of the information became irrelevant (at one point members would see everything their friends 'liked' within the community).

Facebook was forced to deploy increasingly complicated filters (algorithms) to present members the updates they would find most relevant. As a community grows and evolves, its systems grow and evolve too.

The critical lesson, as author Marshall Goldsmith would testify, is *what got you here won't get you there.*[40] To keep learners hooked, to help them get the best information and

---

40   https://www.amazon.com/What-Got-Here-Wont-There/
      dp/0739342231

value from the community, the community needs to constantly reinvent how it helps members get information.

Giansante, for example, can mark questions as 'accepted solutions' if they solve the problem. But every time Dropbox updates its products, changes a feature, or even renames a feature, dozens, or even hundreds, of solutions, which may have worked fine before, no longer work. These obsolete solutions might be those that members find first when they search on Google or in the community. Luckily, Giansante has a process for dealing with this:

> "We bump [add] the outdated answer with an updated link to the real solution. We don't damage the old one, even if it's super dated. We point them to the new one within the old solution."

As Giansante clarifies, they only do that for the biggest threads. It's not feasible to check and update *thousands* of solutions every time a company releases an update.

Most communities begin with community managers like Giansante rolling up their sleeves and manually doing all the work. They remove the bad information and highlight the good. They respond to discussions, point out which questions have been solved, write newsletters to highlight the best activity, and showcase what's popular at any given moment.

During tax season, for example, Squareseller (the community for Square, a payment processing company for small businesses) shows the most common tax-related questions at the top of the page. This is a simple win. If most questions fall within particular topics, showing them in places learners can't miss prevents a lot of confusion. However, there are only so many questions that can appear at the top of the page. Before long, it becomes too overwhelming and a more complex system is needed.

This is where community members can help. StackExchange, for example, allows members to 'flag' bad and outdated posts, which are sent to the person who provided the original answer. It's not a perfect system (s/he may not know the new answer or may no longer be active in the community), but it keeps most responses current or at least shows if the answer no longer works. It even allows some members to update information for themselves. This helps keep the knowledge shared by members in the past useful for members visiting in the future.

Another option is to let members declare what kind of information they want to see and send the information to match. Many platforms, including Twitter, have suggested accounts, hashtopics, or topics to follow. It's a lot easier to send members what they want when they explain what they want. The biggest downside is learners are prone not to sign up or respond in the first place. A more popular option is to let active members highlight the most popular stuff for learners.

This happens on HackerNews, Digg and Facebook through 'liking' and 'upvoting'. Members can highlight the best content in the community, and it naturally rises to the top for learners to see. But this approach also has its own drawbacks. Groups of members soon get together to vote for each other's work. It's also more prone to showing what's popular (cat photos) than what's important (a tsunami in Japan).

A similar approach is known as *trending items:* showing the popular content (by visits or relevant comments) within the past few hours. This keeps the community fresh and provides a reason to visit often, but it's prone to the same problems as upvoting; people cheating the system and visiting what's entertaining more than what's important.

The final and most infamous approach in recent years is to use *algorithms.* Every major platform develops algorithms that show a *tiny percentage* of contributions by members (or the community). But those they do show are the ones anticipated to be most important to each visitor. The downside, as we've seen in recent years, is this leads to *filter bubbles, where members are only exposed to a narrow group of people and ideas,* which can have devastating societal consequences.

No system is foolproof. The right system is the one that matches the size of the community: When we're in the hundreds, we can usually display activity according to when it was posted.

When we're in the thousands, we need editor's picks to highlight the best material.

When we're in the tens of thousands, we need upvoting or self-tagging.

When we're in the hundreds of thousands, we need trending items.

When we're in the millions, we need an algorithm.

Ensuring members can learn easily what they need to learn from your community is absolutely critical to your community becoming indispensable, both to your members and to your organization. Most of the value of a community comes from what members learn. You need to spend time ensuring members are learning what they need to learn as effectively as possible.

Summary

The real value in a community isn't what the tiny percentage of members contribute, it's what the majority of members learn. It's one thing for members to get a solution to a problem. It's another thing entirely to have hundreds of others also benefit from that solution.

Yet members can learn far more than just solutions to problems. They can also learn the latest news, get unique insights and advice to be more successful, and understand the trends and social norms of the sector. The challenge is to identify what your members need to learn, to achieve your goals and ensure you design the entire community to help them learn as effectively as possible. This means applying the right kind of filter.

Without some sort of filter, the amount of information shared in a community quickly becomes overwhelming. Members won't be able to find what they're looking for or they might follow bad advice with disappointing results.

Filters come in several types. These include picking the best stuff manually, letting members vote, using what gets the most clicks, or deploying an algorithm, which uses past behavior to predict what content members are most likely to want to see. The best filters match the size of the community to what information members need to learn. If we get this right, we can make the community indispensable to our learners.

Chapter 5

INSIGHTS

Chris Savage, the CEO of a small video hosting company named Wistia, was momentarily stumped. While reading the analytics of Wistia's latest video, a lighthearted, behind-the-scenes look at the company, he noticed a sudden spike in engagement in its last five seconds.

A rise in interest at the end is almost unheard of. It means *more time* was spent watching the end of the video than the beginning. Typically, a lot of people *drop-off (stop watching)* a video near the beginning and the number levels out over time. This curious anomaly yielded an insight that would propel Wistia from a tiny video hosting business into one of the world's most successful video companies.

Wistia is a video-hosting service launched by two Brown University graduates in 2006. It offers businesses the ability to easily upload, display, and accurately measure engagement in videos. That last feature is key; it's what distinguishes Wistia from YouTube (or what Savage describes as *"the 500 lb gorilla in the room"*). For the past 12 years, Wistia has had to explain why companies should use a paid video hosting service when YouTube is free and more popular.

To answer this simple question and promote Wistia, Savage did what many people did back then, he started a blog. He updated the blog twice a day with creative news. But it wasn't sustainable... and it wasn't working:

> *"It was insane. It was the only thing I was doing. We got to 5,000 email subscribers to this blog. I thought we failed massively."* But this failure, Savage continues, had one major benefit: *"if no-one was reading the blog, why not take some risks with it?"*

Since the six-person company had a strong video background, Savage decided to begin to post some simple, whacky, videos showing the team at work. One of these behind-the-scenes videos became a hit on HackerNews and sent a flood of traffic to Wistia.[41, 42]

> "[the video] *had nothing to do with the product, but it took off,*" Savage adds: "*We did it again and again, more behind-the-scenes content. We had a hit maybe once a quarter.*"

It was one of these videos in which engagement spiked in the final five seconds as the camera pulls back to reveal Wistia's lighting setup. Perhaps, Savage thought, the audience didn't want to learn about Wistia. *They wanted to learn how to set up lighting equipment for themselves.*

It was, to aptly use the phrase, a lightbulb moment.

The comments on the video, questions about the lighting setup, confirmed Savage's suspicion. This insight changed how Wistia marketed themselves. Savage and his team began posting less about the product and the industry and more about how businesses could create their own videos.

First, Wistia created a video on an iPhone to prove businesses don't need professional equipment to make professional-looking videos. The video was an instant hit. Next, Wistia created a tutorial guide on lighting, what content marketers refer to as "*pillar content*"—a definitive piece that attracts a large audience indefinitely via search and referrals. The guide became their breakout article, attracting more traffic than any other resource they had ever posted. Even today, Wistia continues to update it every year with the latest equipment recommendation and tips.

In 2013, Wistia took the next natural step and launched a dedicated library (named the Learning Center). The library of videos covers every major aspect of creating a professional-looking video (lighting, audio, script editing, managing talent,

---

41   https://crlvideo.wistia.com/medias/twgnzr632z
42   https://news.ycombinator.com/item?id=2279856

and plenty more); the center also includes a blog for company news and product updates, videos created by community members, webinars with top experts, and a community based on Slack (a live chat-driven platform). Today, Wistia has six to seven people working full time to develop the learning center.

From six staff and a handful of customers in 2011, Wistia has grown to 400,000 customers across 50 countries. Many of these customers attend WistiaFest, the company's annual conference, to learn the latest tips for creating fantastic videos. All of this results from a single curious anomaly at the end of a video. Wistia is proof that even the tiniest organizations with small communities can stumble upon game-changing insights if they're alert to them.

Every community generates incredible insights every day. Every time someone posts a comment on, votes for, likes something, or clicks a link, they're revealing more about who they are and what they want. Such insights go to waste, like rotting vegetables after the market has closed, unless someone notices. It's a shame, because insights can be transformational. As Savage from Wistia and Allison Leahy at Fitbit discovered, it's relatively easy to track what people are talking about in the community to create content they need. It's just as easy to use a community to ask members what they want or highlight what they are struggling with and what most needs to be fixed.

Insights are the easiest way to get support for a community from peers. As we'll see in this chapter, time and time again, the best value from a community came from insights. Unlike any other community benefit, the value of insights isn't closely correlated with the size of the community. No one needs a huge community to gain huge insights. A community with only a hundred members can find insights just as good as in a community of one million. The challenge is finding them while they're fresh and relevant.

Even better, *members love to give insights*. They love to be asked for their opinion, to have direct access to the brand, to shape the products they use. It helps members feel smart, valuable, and better connected to one another. Savage asked his community to help define the company's mission:

> *"I didn't know what our mission was, so I talked to our community about it. They said we think you help people make their content look good, make stronger connections, and make business more human. The only reason we got this mission was by talking with the community."*

If the last chapter was about what members learn from the community, this chapter is about what we can learn from our members. It's about turning every possible member into a provider of fantastic insights.

Dell lies, Dell sucks

> *I just got a new Dell laptop and paid a fortune for the four-year, in-home service.*
>
> *The machine is a lemon and the service is a lie. I'm having all kinds of trouble with the hardware: overheats, network doesn't work, maxes out on CPU usage. It's a lemon. But what really irks me is that they say if they sent someone to my home—which I paid for—he wouldn't have the parts, so I might as well just send the machine in and lose it for 7-10 days—plus the time going through this crap. So I have this new machine and paid for them to FUCKING FIX IT IN MY HOUSE and they don't and I lose it for two weeks.*
>
> *DELL SUCKS. DELL LIES. Put that in your Google and smoke it, Dell."*
>
> *Jeff Jarvis, 2005[43]*

Jeff Jarvis' prose didn't quite win him a Pulitzer, but his fellow bloggers didn't care. The post attracted 200+ comments and further condemnation of Dell from his peers. If Dell read the post, they made no attempt to respond to it. Despite the comments section being open for business and Jarvis asking (and even taunting) Dell to respond, Dell kept silent.

---

43   https://buzzmachine.com/2005/06/21/dell-lies-dell-sucks/

As the post spread through the blogosphere, Jarvis was invited to write an article for *The Guardian*. He headlined it: "*My Dell Hell*."[44] The phrase stuck. Within six months, Dell's share price tumbled by 25%. Customer sentiment had plunged too. Towards the end of the year, *Business Week* published an article titled "*It's Bad To Worse At Dell*."

Eventually, Dell began to awake from its slumber. In 2005, Dell's technicians began reaching out to bloggers (including Jarvis). The result was so effective, Dell began to launch increasingly more sophisticated initiatives to engage with their customers.

In 2006, Dell launched its own blog (direct2dell), where Dell's newly hired chief blogger, Lionel Menchaca, and others could share the latest updates and interact with customers in the comments. Dell also created a system for their customers to directly rate and review Dell's products on Dell's own site.

StudioDell (a customer video sharing site) followed in 2007, Twitter accounts, and more more blogs (Dell Shares, InsideIT, Small Business blog, and Digital Nomads launched between 2006 and 2008). Accounts on YouTube, Facebook, LinkedIn, Flickr, and most other platforms also were added At their most exuberant, Dell even setup *Dell Island*, a territory within the virtual world Second Life, where users could buy virtual PCs and even order real PCs to play Second Life better.[45] Dell's efforts were rewarded by being named as the #1 Top Social Brand and winning The Altimeter Open Leadership Award for Innovation and Execution.

But among these engagement initiatives, none attracted quite as much attention as *Idea Storm*. Idea Storm is a platform that allows Dell customers to suggest ideas and vote on the ideas they like best. *The Guardian* wrote:

"Dell has done something brilliant: it's launched an IdeaStorm site that enables users to make suggestions so that other

44   https://www.theguardian.com/technology/2005/aug/29/mondaymedia-section.blogging

45   https://www.cnet.com/uk/news/dell-sets-up-second-life-shop-offers-pcs-to-residents/

people can "digg" them. At the moment, there are 141 idea proposals, 1,632 diggs and 146 comments. The two top ideas (there are duplicates) are that Dell should provide the option of a crap-free installation (ie without the junk paid for by Google* and assorted antivirus vendors), and that Dell should "own" green the way Apple "owns" pretty. Not only is Dell tapping into the zeitgeist, it's getting feedback and some good market research."[46]

IdeaStorm wasn't just a hit in the trade press, bloggers loved it too. As one blogger commented:

"Dell's IdeaStorm is the epitome of scalable community-based insight. Dell has opened up every aspect of its operation to end users who in turn provide powerful and original concepts which are later adopted by the company. Dell has gone even further by entrusting its community to decide which ideas should be explored further by employing a simple voting mechanism."[47]

The press loved the idea. Bloggers loved the idea. And members loved the idea!

Ideastorm attracted 6,200 ideas submitted within the first five months, 11 of which were implemented. By October 2015, Dell reported almost 24,000 ideas had been submitted, with 748,010 votes and 100k+ comments. From these, 549 ideas have been implemented. The business metrics are impressive. Dell reported each idea was worth $10k (and *"hundreds of millions of dollars in revenue"*).[48]

On the surface, Dell is a fairytale success story. It's a demonstration of what's possible when an organization solicits ideas

46   https://www.theguardian.com/technology/blog/2007/feb/17/
     dell20michael

47   https://www.liveperson.com/connected-customer/posts/
     power-customer-communities-increasing-roi-through-meaningful-
     engagement

48   https://blog.structure3c.com/2016/09/28/
     beyond-ideas-building-open-innovation-communities/

from its community and implements them. But there is a wrinkle in this fabled story:

When was the last time anyone bought a Dell laptop?

Eight years after since the launch of IdeaStorm, Dell had slipped far behind its competitors. By 2010, Dell claimed the community was generating tens of millions of dollars, but the level of activity had flatlined.

Not all pundits were impressed from the beginning. Jeffrey Phillips, author of multiple books on innovation, explains:

> *"Having a bunch of people submit ideas to a portal is NOT innovation. That is simply a sounding off process, mostly about the problems that exist with current products or perhaps some incremental innovation ideas about how to change the existing products."*[49]

Looking at the list of implemented ideas, it's hard to disagree. There aren't any game-changers in the bunch. There's no new iPhone or iPod here. The most popular ideas include keeping XP on Dell systems, national call centers, backlit keyboards, optional preinstalled software (which contradicts other ideas), sales pages organized by need, etc... All of these are ideas focused on incremental improvement (or were borrowed from competitors). It's hard to believe most of these ideas weren't already on Dell's roadmap. *Forbes* highlighted the real problem with community insights :

> *"The jury's also out on whether IdeaStorm reflects the opinions of the average Dell buyer. Many of the site's most popular ideas involve adding the open-source Linux operating system instead of Windows. If IdeaStorm votes were a true gauge of customers, Linux PCs should be flying off the shelves. They're not."*[50]

---

49   http://innovateonpurpose.blogspot.co.uk/2008/05/why-ideastorm-and-salesforce-ideas-are.html

50   http://archive.fortune.com/2008/09/03/technology/fortt_dell.fortune/index.htm

Many people interviewed for this book cited Dell as an example of an innovation success story, but none could name a single innovative idea the community came up with (and none of them owned any Dell products). IdeaStorm shows both the great promise of asking customers to directly share great ideas and the challenges of doing it. These challenges come in three forms. First, crowdsourced ideas can easily resemble a list of customer complaints. *Isn't every complaint also an idea to improve?* A group of engineers or customer support may be able to come up with an idea equally as good (if not better).

The second is the quality of ideas. Most aren't great. Customers don't know the constraints Dell operates under or Dell's broader strategy, which makes it hard to come up with a useful idea. Even if a member had presciently suggested in 2007 Dell should sell its hardware division, launch a streaming music service, or start a 3D printing division, it's hard to imagine Dell would have listened. The ideas would have seemed ridiculous.

This doesn't mean ideation itself is a bad idea. It means there is a huge difference between soliciting ideas and getting insights from those ideas.

Forth

In 2008, Local Motors hit a home run with the *The Rally Fighter*, a new car designed and built by the community.[51] Seeing a trend towards 'co-creation', Local Motors launched a platform, Launch Forth, to crowdsource ideas from engineers. The idea is similar to Kaggle: companies pay a fee to set challenges and crowdsource ideas from 40,000+ designers, engineers, and technologists to shape the future of their industries. Current challenges range from the visionary '*designing cities on Mars*'[52] to the more immediate '*detecting erosion under insulated pipes.*'[53]

---

51 Quite literally, members work together in groups to assemble the car.
52 https://launchforth.io/hpmars/
   mars-home-planet-3d-modeling-challenge/brief/
53 https://launchforth.io/launchforth/detecting-corrosion-under-
   insulation/latest/

Local Motors suffers from the same challenges faced by Dell. The level of participation and the quality of ideas varies enormously by challenge. Worse, few of the ideas ever seem to be implemented. But this is where it gets interesting. According to Brenton Murray, Launch Forth's community manager, projects are less about ideas and more about the insights:

> *"Sometimes it's [setting a challenge] done as an internal exercise to inject new ideas and fresh approaches into the organization. Sometimes it's meant to validate what the engineering team are already doing. Sometimes it's just to get the current engineering team to rethink how they approach things. Not all of the ideas are designed to be built, they're designed to change how people think."*

Ideas are interesting, but the insights are indispensable. Insights can validate a company's way of thinking, identify new opportunities, or change how they think about a problem. Even bad ideas can yield good insights. Almost any community can do the same thing.

For example, FeverBee could launch a competition for members to suggest ways of growing our community practice. We could set rewards of $1000, $2500, and $5000 for the top three ideas as voted by members of our community. Our community isn't huge, but if we get 30 to 50 ideas, that would be enough to see if we're on the right track, missing any obvious opportunities, or could be doing anything better. Even validating what we already believe would be a useful insight. If any of the insights *within* these ideas leads to just one client, or stops us wasting time in just one area, it's paid for itself many times over.

This is what Murray means when he suggests it doesn't always matter if the idea is implemented or not. By going outside of an organization, especially to a community of 40,000 engineers, Murray believes a company can escape its own tunnel vision. Ideas can identify the pulse of the industry, the latest technology, and new approaches that otherwise might never have been considered. Clearly, there are some truly terrible ideas on Forth, but it doesn't matter—what matters are insights.

Ideas, however, are just one method to get members to deliver insights. Another more common approach is to ask for feedback.

FeverBee

On August 21, 2017, I published a short blog post looking for help with this book:[54]

A total of 36 people responded and were invited to a separate group in the FeverBee Community (for community professionals, it's very meta). Members went through each draft of every chapter and gave their feedback. Not all of it was easy to read, but it was immensely valuable. Some would give feedback on an entire chapter within hours. Community members refined the book's theme, advised which chapters to remove, clarified key points, and provided plenty of useful examples (feel free to blame them if the book is terrible!).

In the past few years, FeverBee hasn't launched any major project without first getting the feedback of members. We call this *battle testing*. If members love it, great. If they don't, we make changes until they do. Our entire approach is to avoid firing blanks. If something doesn't resonate with members, we're wasting everyone's time.

Gathering feedback on products or ideas is the easiest (and often most effective) way to get great insights from a community. It doesn't require a huge audience, just a dozen or more people willing to share their opinions. Most importantly, *members want to help*. Community members enjoy giving feedback, feeling their expertise is valued, and feeling they had an impact. Where else can members change the very products they use? This is one of the clearest areas where a brand community can offer value members can't get anywhere else. Members can see how they're shaping the products used by thousands, if not millions, of people.

There are many ways to get feedback from a community. Members can give feedback on products, marketing efforts, website design, work processes, and more. It's so easy to do,

---

54   https://www.FeverBee.com/book/

it's almost negligent *not* to regularly ask the community for feedback. However, there is a big problem with solicited feedback, a problem that can lead many organizations to spend a lot of time on problems members don't really care about.

Why Complaints Are Great

In 2016, we began working with a client who had an infinite number of feature problems to solve and a limited number of engineers to solve them. These engineers also had a lot of autonomy. They were free (to a large degree) to work on whichever project would let them have the biggest impact. Their challenge was *identifying* which problems would have the biggest impact. For example, should they resolve a minor frustration on a feature used by the majority of members or undertake a massive improvement on a product used by a minority of members?

The easiest solution would be to ask members for their opinions. But this would show us what members *think* about a problem, not whether they *care* about the problem. In an episode of the TV show *The West Wing*, a democratic pollster tries to persuade the President to come out strongly in favour of a flag burning amendment. His numbers show 80% of people support the amendment.

Later in the episode, another pollster, Joey Lucas, explains the poll shows a *position* on an issue, but not the degree to which they *care* about the issue. Only 37% of the 80% said they rated it important or very important, and just 12% of this group (about 3.5% of the population) said it would swing their vote.

This is true in communities too. Community members might tell a car company they prefer a large cup holder, but the size of the cup holder won't sway their decision to buy the car. Likewise, very few people bought *The Rally Fighter*, the very car they had designed. So, instead, we needed to look at unsolicited feedback: when a customer cares so strongly about the issue they have taken the time to visit a community to give that feedback. We're all very familiar with one form of unsolicited feedback, *complaints*.

Complaints are valuable. When someone takes the initiative, time, and effort to post a complaint, they care about it enough to sway their decisions. However, most brands are already getting plenty of complaints (or *feedback*) through their existing customer support channels. When we worked with Facebook, for example, the number of complaints posted in the community was *dwarfed* by the number Facebook received through other channels. Why bother listening to complaints in a community compared with those through other channels?

Complaints posted in a community typically have four major benefits. First, they offer insight into what the best and most passionate customers are thinking. If they're unhappy, it can portend an impending PR crisis, often one led by a brand's top customers.

In April 2018, Which? announced it would be closing its free email service. The email service had launched in 1997, but had ceased accepting new accounts in 2004. It remained active, but the technology was becoming increasingly outdated and the number of users had dwindled to a few thousand active accounts. Unable to keep supporting the platform, Which? announced users would have two months to find a different provider[55].

The backlash from members of Which?'s community was immediate and ferocious. It's difficult enough for technically proficient people to move information from one email account to another. For Which?'s members, comprised largely of an older demographic (60+) who hadn't needed to tweak their email settings for 20+ years, it would prove extremely stressful. Worse yet, many members relied on their Which.net email accounts for vital communications from doctors and hospitals.

Which?'s community members didn't just restrict their outrage to the community, but proactively pushed the story (and were happily quoted) in newspapers,[56] trade press,[57] and other media.

---

55 And a FeverBee client.
56 https://www.theguardian.com/money/2018/apr/15/
which-consumers-association-email-internet-closing
57 https://www.theregister.co.uk/2018/04/03/
which_to_shutter_ageing_email_service/

Eventually Which? agreed to provide better support for every member who needed to move an email address and provide email forwarding to any other account for an additional six months[58]. This added temporary relief to the immediate problem, but rebuilding member's trust in the organization will take far longer.

Community members aren't representative of any brand's entire customer base, but they do represent the best, most passionate, and most informed audiences. They represent the audience a brand least wants to antagonize.

The second benefit of complaints in a community is they can be responded to with more freedom and empathy than they would receive through standard customer support tickets. The number of complaints is lower and they bring their history of previous interactions and information. Customers can get better responses than they would through any other channel.

The third benefit is that a (public) community is available for anyone to access and utilize at any time. Within some companies, access to internal resources and data can be tricky. But the community is right there for any group to correlate their activities with member sentiment whenever they need. Dropbox's Giansante described this well:

> "We have a standard of how many people click on our desktop client every day. If we suddenly see a drop of 20% we will check the community to see if there are any comments or anything which is broken and try to correlate the metric change in what's happening in the community."

This provides both an easy source of contextual data (it's often easier for engineers to instantly access the community than peruse customer support tickets) and reveals the sentiment. The community feedback has become so critical that, according to Giansante, there is someone from the engineering team checking the community all day long:

> "We have 2 to 3 releases per week but we're not releasing the new version to every user [...] we zero in on the community

---

58   https://conversation.which.co.uk/discussions/
      which-net-discussion-area/

threads for each person, which thread relates to each version of Dropbox.

Each engineer can focus on feedback from specific users on specific updates. This provides terrific contextual data to let engineers work rapidly to improve the product.

The final and most important benefit is complaints can be aggregated to show priorities. If we had asked our client's community members what they wanted us to work on, we risked getting a list of ideas that might not influence their behavior. Instead, we began looking at the complaints posted in the community and used the most frequent topics to build a roadmap of priorities. It let engineers see what to work on to have the biggest fewer possible impact (it also let them track the results of their work: fewer complaints about that feature).

Each of these benefits is useful to both members and the brand. They help members get better responses, feel like they were listened to, and they influence the brand itself. While complaints are the most popular type of unsolicited feedback, they're far from the only feedback. Another type of feedback lies in the sentiment and the words members choose to use.

It's possible to get a unique insight into community members and what they're thinking through their tone of voice and word choices. It's possible to build member profiles to feedback to staff who can use this data. This ensures the brand uses the words to match terms members use to describe problems. For example, a question in the Facebook community was how to report the death of a relative. The member had searched but couldn't find an answer. Why not? Because Facebook used the phrase *memorialize*. Today, Facebook has improved the wording to include terms like 'deceased relative' on the relevant help page.

This type of information can change how a brand names areas of the website, what's included in the FAQ, and the language they use to attract search traffic. Ultimately, every piece of feedback (complaints, questions, or sentiment) is an opportunity to learn more about features members really care about and how to keep them happy. It's both an early warning system and a chance to resolve major problems.

Counting Clicks

If Which? faced a storm from its community, Facebook faced a tsunami, hurricane, and earthquake all rolled into one when it launched its most synonymous feature, *the news feed*.

As Mark Kirkpatrick, explained in his book *The Facebook Effect*, over 500 protest groups were set up in the days after the introduction of the news feed. Approximately 10% of the site's membership actively protested the change. It wasn't long before the largest, oldest groups on the site were those set up to protest against the news feed (which had enabled them to grow rapidly).

But Facebook CEO Mark Zuckerberg did something remarkable. He stood his ground. Beyond a few tweaks to help members protect their privacy, he decided to ride out the storm. As Kirkpatrick describes, Zuckerberg had the data on his side.

> *"But Zuckerberg, in fact, knew that people liked the News Feed, no matter what they were saying in the groups. He had the data to prove it. People were spending more time on Facebook, on average, than before News Feed launched. And they were doing more there—dramatically more. In August, users viewed 12 billion pages on the service. But by October, with News Feed underway, they viewed 22 billion".*

If the problem with solicited feedback is it gives opinions, the problem with unsolicited feedback is often members don't know what they want. As Kirkpatrick paraphrases Zuckerberg: *"users take time to get used to changes, no matter how inevitable or necessary they might seem."*

It's impossible to imagine the psychological impact of millions of members setting up groups to protest against us, calling for our resignation, and attacking us personally. As we've seen with Ellen Pao at Reddit, it can make a CEO's position untenable. It's critical to look at the data in these situations. Members might say they dislike a feature, but does the data support that?

Every single click in the community yields a new insight. Clicks reveal trends, areas of concern, and what members really want.

Data can reveal what brings newcomers to the brand community in the first place. It's possible to extract powerful insights from this data. Working with our client, Eventbrite, we tracked a sharp increase in visits to a discussion on GDPR compliance for event professionals (a new European regulation covering data privacy). While the post was getting more visits, it wasn't getting more comments. A lot of people had the same question, but few had the right answers. This was a huge opportunity. We asked members to share their templates, brought in a top legal expect to host a live Q&A session, and attracted a huge number of new members—all from tracking the rising popularity of visits to a single discussion.

If you track the top 50 discussions/activities within the community by landing page each month, you should be able to see which topics are rising and falling in popularity. While most will remain relatively the same, those that rise and fall by a significant amount warrant a closer look. That data highlights areas for developing new content, problems you need to solve, or new audiences you might want to target.

Community data might also show a rising number of visits from a geographic region, so you could start translating product content for that region. A rising number of visits from specific websites might reveal companies and authors you can bring into an official partner program. It can also show visits from people on different devices. Consider developing apps for those devices. Every click reveals an insight. No one should act on a single data point, but it can certainly confirm or refute any assumptions. Members might not tell the truth in polls, interviews, or surveys, but data doesn't lie.

Data doesn't just help the brand, it helps its members too when their clicks are used to provide a better experience for them. The challenge is interpreting the results correctly. A former client, a mental health charity, once came to the conclusion their audience of young adults (13 to 24) were most interested in questions relating to sex. This "insight" came from observing the majority of visitors arrived at pages related to teenagers asking questions about sex. What they didn't notice was visitors to these topics had a 100% bounce rate and stayed on these pages for less than 3 seconds. This probably wasn't the audience they wanted to attract.

Summary

The insights generated by a community are too valuable to waste. The easiest way to make any community more valuable to any brand is to be better at harnessing the insights it creates. Today, most insights rot away because they're not tracked or well used. A truly indispensable community excels at generating insights the rest of the organization finds invaluable.

These insights come in many forms as we see below.

		COMPANY	
		SOLICITED	UNSOLICITED
MEMBERS	AWARE	**Ideas and opinions** Includes ideation, co-creation, surveys, polls interviews, asking for ideas and feedback *e.g. asking customers what they think about a product.*	**Complaints** Includes problem posts, voting on problems (or 'me too') posts *e.g. waiting to see what customers think about a product.*
	UNAWARE	**Sentiment** Includes tracking mentions and popularity of topics. It involves identifying the words and language members use *e.g. waiting to see what your best customers say about a product.*	**Clicks** Click-through rates, conversion rates, attribution, landing page data *e.g. tracking what people are most interested in about the product.*

Insight can be solicited or unsolicited. Any brand can create a competition and ask their members for ideas to solve it. The ideas themselves might not be fantastic, but they can lead to game-changing insights. A brand can also ask for feedback on existing products and services, which gives an immediate way of seeing what members prefer in any situation. But be careful of mistaking someone's opinion on an issue with how much they care about it. For this we need to look at unsolicited feedback.

Complaints are the most common type of feedback. Complaints are incredibly valuable. Not only can they be resolved in the community with deep empathy for every member, they can highlight what members most care about and help develop priorities in the future. But what members say doesn't always match what they do. We need to track clicks too. Where do members come from, what do they click on, what do they read? The number of possible insights is infinite.

Every community is an insight-generating machine. As a community grows, it can develop better and better insights. A community might be launched to generate ideas or deflect calls, but it can quickly expand to asking for feedback and what's most popular. This hits strongly at a member's need for competence, at the opportunity to experience mastery and a feeling of success in what they do. When members feel successful, they start to see the community as indispensable.

Chapter 6

EDUCATE & SUPPORT

In late 1999, Dave Garrett, director of knowledge management for a global IT firm, had an epiphany:

'What if a project manager could easily access all of the tools a large consulting firm had available via a website?'

Garrett, a veteran of the project management industry, knew the industry was dominated by consultancy firms who hoarded the best resources and charged fees most project managers could never afford. Yet, every project manager had access to (or had developed) their own in-house templates and resources. Some of these tools were as good as any large consulting firm's (most project managers are self-employed or working solo at a company). If there were a place to pool these high-quality resources together, everyone would benefit[59].

1999 was still the early days of online communities. The technology and social norms that make communities successful didn't exist. Building a place where people would voluntarily share their best information in the pre-Wikipedia days seemed nuts.

Garrett could have taken the usual route and created every resource himself. But he was just one man with a single, narrow set of experiences compared to the collective wisdom of thousands of his peers. The real value would be getting others to share their best stuff.

In 2000, Garrett launched a new online publication for project managers called Gantthead[60]. Gantthead's goal was to

---

59   https://www.marketingsherpa.com/article/interview/
     how-to-reach-250000-it
60   At the time, most project managers still used Gantt charts.

make project managers more successful. Garrett wanted it to be a place developed by project managers *for* project managers, a place to connect hundreds of thousands of isolated project managers around the world. It would feature the best resources from the smartest people. But, if Gantthead was going to work, Garrett would have to overcome one obvious problem: *How do you get the smartest people in a profession to share their best resources with their biggest competitors?*

Anyone who has ever tried to persuade people to pool resources stumbles across what's known as the *public goods* problem. In economics, the *public goods* problem occurs when the cost of creating the '*public good*' (e.g. high-quality resource) falls upon the few (creators) but the benefits are dispersed across the many (readers). A rational actor (member) in such a system (a community) is best served by free-riding (reading without contributing). This is exactly what most community members do: they learn without contributing.

One way to tackle this problem is to force everyone to contribute (i.e. a member must share to access high-quality resource from others). The burden is dispersed across the many, but it's prone to people sharing poor-quality resources to get access to better ones. A more effective approach is to change the equation. Reward the creators with something more valuable than the cost of creating the resource, usually money.

Contributors are paid more than the cost of creating the resource. But, with some exceptions, money doesn't flow so well through a community. Readers aren't usually willing to pay enough to truly compensate the creators for their time. Creators want to be compensated with something even more valuable than the financial rewards readers are willing to cough up; they need to be paid in *reputation.*

Usually shining a spotlight upon the best contributions works well. Members get the reputation points and learners get the best resources. The problems with such an approach are, a) there might not be many submissions in the first place, or b) there aren't enough good submissions to choose from. It's easy to end up shining the spotlight on subpar submissions and bad contributions beget more bad contributions.

Instead of asking everyone to submit their best resources and hope the best would stand out, Garrett only accepted high-quality resources. He was betting that, if having a submission accepted was difficult, only the smartest people would share their resources.

An academic journal works similarly. If getting an article published is a hallmark of success, it's where successful people want to be (regardless of how few people read academic articles). Of course, he risked not receiving many submissions. He also risked upsetting members by rejecting their lovingly-crafted submissions.

So Garrett put together a simple criteria. First, every resource had to be new (not previously published elsewhere). This prevented Gantthead from falling victim to the LinkedIn trap (members dumping content they've posted elsewhere). Second, every resource had to be approved by editors of the site. The criteria was loose enough to encourage enough people to submit resources, but firm enough to reject those that didn't make the grade. Most importantly, it worked. Getting a resource accepted on Gantthead became a mark of expertise and the foundation of building a reputation within the field.

The community has also awarded members an *influence* score for their contributions. The score, between 1 and 100, is based upon how widely a member's content is shared, whether members ask questions that generate a lot of discussion, and how well members are expanding and engaging with their network. The score is broken down into different categories of activity where members most often participate.

Garrett has a predictably high influence score of 70, but also a score of 45 on communications management, 31 on strategy, and 26 on portfolio management.[61] As a member's influence score increases, they can participate in specific activities, like creating content, participating at conferences, and becoming a chapter leader (managing their own group). The community taps strongly into a member's need for competence and building a reputation. The Project Management Institute's

---

61   https://www.projectmanagement.com/profile/dgarrett

(PMI) Marjorie Anderson explains that it also provides a sense of autonomy.

Growing the reputations of top members grows their egos too. Top experts become increasingly protective over their resources. As a result, PMI has been forced to take a *very* light editorial touch. While PMI filters for quality and provide feedback, they generally ensure documents appear almost as they are shared. They don't fiddle with them. Any member can propose an idea and get good feedback from a paid editorial team, but the final resource, with a very few light corrections (mostly spelling/grammar), is all a contributor's work. This sense of autonomy, Anderson believes, is critical to attracting further contributions.

Today the community has 800k+ members who have created 14,000 articles and over 1,000 templates in four areas: deliverables, project plans, presentations, and checklists. Access to this high-quality library of member-created resources is now one of the major benefits of joining the Project Management Institute. The best resources from the community are even featured on the company's homepage.

If Garrett had followed the conventional approach, he would have launched a community for people to talk about project management and hope members shared good advice. It's *always* easier in the short-term to drive members to discussion boards and ask them to talk about the relevant issues of the day. This would have driven a lot of engagement but it would be ephemeral at best. A single good template or resource is worth thousands of comments and opinion posts. Instead, he followed the hard path that made the community *indispensable* to his members.

Getting Top Members To Contribute Their Best Work

The experts who share their best resources in Garrett's PMI community are outliers. They represent the rarefied and treasured group of people who have the time, expertise, and passion to contribute huge major resources to the community. They're willing to put their projects into the world knowing everyone can see them and anyone can criticize them. Only a tiny percentage of members ever do this in any community. The rest don't have the time, expertise, and passion to share. They need all three. Members with only time and passion create bad resources. Members with expertise and passion are too busy to take on extra work. Members with only time and expertise aren't interested in sharing their best resources. It's almost impossible to shift these fundamentals. But we can work with them.

Almost every client FeverBee has had believes their audience is too busy to participate. But members can still make great contributions if they're asked to do the right things. Members might not be able to share in as much detail as PMI's members do, but they can still share links, blog posts, leave reviews, news, or their opinions. Figure1, a community of doctors, makes it simple for members to participate. All they need to do is take out their phone, take a photo of an X-ray of a patient's condition, and share it.

Once we know how much time, expertise, and passion members have, it becomes easier, as in the table below, to determine what we may ask members to do:

	Time	Expertise	Passion
Templates and resources	X	X	X
Blog posts	X	X	X
Tips		X	X
Solutions		X	X
Reviews		X	X
Sharing links / news			X
Connections			X
Opinions			

Every member can be pushed to make a more valuable contribution. The above table shows the relative value of each type of contribution. Resources are at the top and opinions at the bottom. It doesn't take much time, expertise, or passion to share an opinion. Opinions aren't usually very valuable to most members who visit a community. Resources, however, directly save people a lot of time and money.

For most communities, the real effort is in getting members to share blog posts, tips, solutions, reviews, links, and connections. The higher up the value chain members go, the more valuable the community becomes.

The Biggest Rock Stars On Spotify

Spotify, a music streaming service, needed a solution to their customer support problem. The company's user base was rapidly outgrowing their customer support team. When Spotify launched in 2008, it had a few hundred thousand active users and almost no paying customers. By mid-2011, 10m+ users and at least 1.5m paying subscribers were on Spotify.[62] Spotify was about to encounter its biggest challenge: *to open registration in North America.*

The entire valuation of a startup is based upon the idea it can scale and sustain healthy profit margins. Scaling isn't the same as growth. Growth means acquiring customers and spending more money to support those customers. As a restaurant chain grows, for example, it obviously needs to hire more staff, buy more food, and incur more overheads. Scaling, however, means acquiring more customers while keeping associated expenses low. It doesn't cost Facebook, Amazon, or Google much to support one additional customer.

However, the more customers a company acquires, the more questions they're likely to have. The more questions, the more support staff a company needs to ensure members receive good answers. These are exactly the kinds of costs that prevent a company from scaling. By the time Spotify was ready to launch in North America, in 2011, the company had millions of customers to support but limited budget to hire a global

---

62   https://www.statista.com/statistics/244995/
      number-of-paying-spotify-subscribers/

support team. Spotify came up with a solution we've seen work repeatedly: they would build a support community.

It's simple enough to give customers a place to ask questions and share complaints. But why would anyone want to volunteer their spare time to give free customer support? Spotify's new Global Community Manager, Rorey Jones, faced that challenge. Soon after Jones' arrival, he took notice of an interesting fact. Spotify didn't have thousands of members each sharing their own nuggets of wisdom and solving problems; Spotify had a tiny group of members responding to a large number of questions:

"I remember the very first power user we had, and this is way before we had any dedicated headcount, platform or community resources," Jones explained. *"When we would launch a new feature and someone from the community had a question, we noticed there was a user with the username 'Spotify's Little Helper' who wasn't really being asked to answer any of these questions yet there he was, helpful and excited about sharing his knowledge and passion for Spotify. At one point, someone from our team suggested that we do something to reward him and so we upgraded his account to premium. That was really the genesis of "community" at Spotify, and it has only evolved from there."*[63]

Actually, it wasn't so much the genesis of a community as as it was one of the most successful superuser programs.

A superuser program is essentially a mixed reward scheme. Members of the community are encouraged and rewarded for helping other people in the community. The more questions a member answers, the greater the rewards. Like frequent flyer miles or any loyalty scheme, members enjoy escalating tiers of benefits. Some benefits are tangible (free Fitbit trackers), others are intangible (status badges).

In November 2013, Spotify capitalized upon its small group of users and launched its *Rock Star Program*.[64] Begun as a program

63   https://www.linkedin.com/pulse/
     community-20-interview-rorey-jones-global-manager-spotify-briant/
64   https://community.spotify.com/t5/Community-Blog/
     Spotify-Community-Rock-Star-Program/ba-p/580948

to recognize awesome contributors and let them earn points for helping out, the goal wasn't to drive engagement. Jones knew that engagement was a redundant metric. The goal was to get great responses to community questions.

The program, like ProjectManagement.com, was exclusive by nature (a common theme). Community members with at least 10 posts could apply to join. Once a member had joined, they could earn points for every answer they provided to a question. Points could be redeemed for premium codes, Spotify gear, music equipment, or access to playlists.

Jones soon discovered his members were far more motivated by *special access.* They wanted to feel a sense of autonomy and competence by getting access to exclusive news, test new products, or just feel involved in the future of music's fastest growing business. Intrinsic rewards (curiosity, connection, exploration) trumped simple, tangible, extrinsic rewards. Better yet, intrinsic rewards were cheaper.

Spotify's Rock Stars are a mixture of power users (product experts) and super users (most active members) who respond to questions from members, help filter great ideas, suggest their own ideas, participate in monthly podcasts, and give feedback on advanced versions of Spotify's products. Their feedback has real consequences.

For example, the popular '*repeat one song*' feature is one of many ideas that originated in the community. Among the tiny group of Rock Stars is an even more exclusive group, the *elite Rock Stars.* Every year the top ten contributors are flown to the company's headquarters in Stockholm to participate in Rock Star Jam, a reward for the best members. It's a status-building exercise and helps Spotify gain valuable insights from their very best customers.

While most programs try to enroll as many people as possible, Spotify seeks out the few members with the magical blend of free time and passion for the product. They set them high objectives and work with them to create thousands of solutions. The Rock Star program remains a relatively small group of 120 to 150 rockstars. But this small group contributes a lot.

In February 2016, Spotify announced the Rock Star program had contributed 158,000 posts in total (around 1,000 posts each).[65] This included 68% (12,600) of the 18,535 *accepted solutions* within the community.[66] Overall, the top 0.0036% of members providing 68% of the most valuable activity (and the single top member alone has contributed over 47,000 posts to the community over a few years).

The Rock Star program, as Jones explains, is undoubtedly the key pillar to supporting Spotify's community of 6.4m members worldwide.[67] However, it's not just the community members who benefit from the efforts of Spotify's Rock Stars, it's the entire 140m+ customer base. The value in fostering a tiny army of highly active supporters lies not only in what they do on the community platform but what they do off the platform, too.

Most of Spotify's customers will never visit the community. Even if they have a problem, they're as likely to ask a question on Facebook, Twitter, Quora, Reddit, or a dozen or more platforms that may have risen or fallen since this book was published. The magic of Spotify's Rock Stars is they don't only answer questions on the community site but also on social media channels, Q&A sites, and even other forums.

Spotify even created an @AskRockStars Twitter handle, which sends messages directly to 120 people within the program. Now people can get answers from people like themselves—ideally even faster than on any official support channel. Once superusers begin answering questions outside as well as inside the community, their value grows exponentially. As we saw with Fitbit, a community doesn't end at the walls of a website, it extends to anyone who feels they are a part of it. At Spotify,

---

65   https://community.spotify.com/t5/Community-Blog/
     CONTEST-Four-Years-of-the-Spotify-Community/ba-p/1287781
66   An accepted solution is an answer to a question marked by the poster
     or by a staff member as the best way to resolve a problem. This allows
     people to find the answer to their question without reading every
     response to the question.
67   At time of writing, Jan, 2018.

as well as Fitbit, they answer questions in as many places as possible.

Jones' Rock Star program might be one of the most successful, but it's just one of *many* superuser, top contributor, or MVP (most valuable person) programs. Most major customer support communities have some form of recognition program. People who have the expertise, time, and passion to answer countless questions from members are unique and special. It's an appreciation that these people aren't driven by money, they're driven by interest.

Programs like Jones' do have one obvious limitation. They need a large number of provocative questions to answer. Superusers don't usually proactively share knowledge—they need a question to answer. Their expertise falls within that singular category of what members know they don't know (*'the known unknowns'*). That's great if a member is trying to get the Spotify app to work on a phone, but it's not so great if they've just bought a $2,000 food processor and aren't sure what to do with it.

Vorwerk

In 2009, Vorwerk[68] decided to *'bring their Thermomix customers home'*.

The Thermomix is the swiss army knife of food processors. The single device can weigh, chop, blend, mix, grind, grate, cook, steam, whisk, and knead food. It has a color touchscreen and a handy side-chip to gather recipes. The Thermomix also has a cult fan base who love to exchange recipes.

Until 2009, recipes were spread across Facebook and popular cooking sites. Vorwerk decided to give their customers a proper home for their recipes. Following Spotify's path, they launched a forum. As with many similar brands, they soon discovered forums are great platforms for members to answer each other's questions, but they are not useful for members to proactively share tips and recipes.

---

68   Vorwerk is a FeverBee client.

Forums require questions to get answers. But sharing a recipe doesn't begin with a question, it begins with personal exploration. Vorwerk soon realized their forum wasn't working and rebuilt a community site designed solely for members to share recipes. The new site closely mirrored recipe cookbooks. Members were invited to share large photos, a list of ingredients, and their step by step instructions (which involved the Thermomix). Members can comment on each other's recipes, but the focus is on sharing recipes.

The new site proved to be an instant hit. Regional groups began first in Australia and soon spread to Italy, Spain, Portugal, Germany, the UK, and many other countries. Each new regional community attracted a large following of customers eager to share their best recipes. Today, a fan base of 150,000 members has shared over 180,000 recipes. Most importantly, as Michelle Aggiato, Head of Social Communication (and Customer Love) at Vorwerk notes, the community attracts a phenomenal 2.5m visitors *every week*.

Aggiato credits Vorwerk's success to three important factors. The first, Aggiato explains, is to have a brand that sells directly to customers, especially a product customers care a great deal about. As Fitbit's Allison Leahy alluded to earlier, customers are far more likely to share tips for a product they love (and which costs more than $2,000) than for a brand that sells something they don't love. There aren't many 'can opener' communities in the world.

The second factor is to recognize and build upon existing behavior. It makes sense to create a place for members to share tips when they're already doing so. It's always harder to create a new behavior from scratch. If members aren't already sharing tips, it's usually because they don't have the expertise or (more likely) the passion to do it.

The third factor is to design for the behavior the company wants. This is the much overlooked secret of tip-sharing (and almost any kind of community contribution outside of Q&A). If members proactively share a lot of great tips and advice, the website should be designed for that.

A community for writers might focus on sharing short stories and letting members mark up the copy with their feedback. An exercise community might encourage members to share stats and clips of their workouts. This is more expensive, but pays off many times over. . A total of 180,000 recipes adds a lot of value to the Thermomix. The greater variety of meals members can cook on the Thermomix, the more valuable it becomes. Since the community's relaunch, sales of the Thermomix have risen from just over 500m euros in 2010 to just under 1.3bn euros by 2016[69].

Recipes are equally useful to someone who has been using the Thermomix for years as someone who bought one yesterday. In other situations, however, the value of tips varies. As Adobe's community will show us, there is a huge difference in the value of tips for beginners and top experts.

Adobe Photoshop Community

Karen Schneider[70] joined the Adobe community and posted her first comment on August 3, 2012. Between September 2012 and April 2014, Schneider posted 10 short tips in Adobe's Photoshop community. Then, as mysteriously as she arrived, Schneider vanished and hasn't returned to the community since.

Her tips, which couldn't be more simple, almost certainly generated more value to Adobe than Schneider will ever know. She collated advice from across the web to answer the most basic questions, including *"How do I open my photo in Photoshop?"* *"How do I crop or trim my photo?"* and *"How do I get rid of Red Eye in my photo?"*.

No self-respecting Photoshop expert would waste their time answering such simple questions. After all, who's going to be impressed by someone explaining how to open a photo in

---

69 https://corporate.vorwerk.com/fileadmin/data/master_corporate/04_Presse/Publikationen/Vorwerk-Corporate-Presentation-2018.pdf

70 I've never met or spoken with Karen. Her tips were one of many I could have used as an example for the book.

Photoshop? The answer, of course, is a first-time photoshop user and a lot more first-time users than experts exist.

Using Photoshop for the first time is intimidating. The jump from fiddling with some free tool (remember Paint?) to software like Photoshop is like jumping from a bicycle into the cockpit of a jumbo jet. We have the most powerful set of photo imaging tools at our fingertips, but no idea how to use them.

Companies like Adobe lose a lot of people in the trial stage. The software is too overwhelming. This is where contributions like Schneider's are so powerful. Collectively, Schneider's beginner-level tips have been seen by hundreds of thousands of Photoshop users. They're still featured in the Frequently Asked Questions of the Photoshop Beginners forum (October 2017).

Even if we conservatively estimate just 1% of viewers continued to use Photoshop because they found Schneider's tips at their most frustrating moment, this would be an additional thousand paying customers ($120 per year). In short, Schneider's brief time in the community is probably contributing a six-figure plus sum annually to the company.

While $120k per year is admittedly a rounding error to a $6bn-a-year company like Adobe, Schneider is just *one* member sharing a *handful* of tips in a *single* part of the community (the Adobe *Beginners* Photoshop community). Consider Adobe has a dozen communities on Photoshop alone and several dozen communities for other products, each with thousands of members sharing advice, and you can start to imagine the incredible value of sharing tips in the community. Once we include any customers who might upgrade and subscribe to other products in the Adobe family, the value begins to multiply.

The biggest obstacle preventing members from sharing tips is a perceived lack of expertise. Most people don't consider themselves *qualified* to share their advice. They're worried other people will suggest a better solution or criticize what they've said. It's easier for every member to wait for a question to answer than proactively share something they've learnt. It takes a particular kind of person to give unsolicited advice audience and not worry the audience will boo them off the community.

Another problem, as we've seen with ProjectManagement. com, is that most people share expertise to boost their status. There isn't much glory in telling members how to open a photo. Yet it's the beginner-level questions that offer the most value. The most advanced advice only appeals to a small group of elite members who are already a brand's most loyal and passionate customers.

So despite beginners comprising the majority of people in most communities, it's hard to get people to share beginner-level advice. For Adobe Photoshop and most other companies, these are the most valuable kinds of tips a member can share because it stops people leaving when they find the learning curve too steep.

Adobe created a specific category for Photoshop Beginners, a clear place for tips to be shared. The best tips are posted prominently open on the community landing page (the first page people arrive to within the Photoshop community). This sends a great signal. If anyone submits a really great tip for beginners, they can be featured too! Adobe gets lucky by the law of large numbers. With so many customers, at least a few will share beginner tips.

Another way to get people to share beginner-level expertise is to list the kind of tips the community most needs or let members request what they want. One of PMI's unique innovations is to ask members to propose ideas for new templates that they personally don't have the expertise to create. These are usually very specific; for example, "*Sample RFP for Replacing an Information System*" or "*Effort-based Forecasting Workbook*". This is the midway point between a question that needs a response and a proactively shared tip. It nudges members when and where to share advice and guides the focus to newcomer-level material.

Even with nudging, most members still find the act of proactively sharing a tip requires a little more expertise than they possess. But this doesn't mean members have nothing to contribute. They can still share great expertise from elsewhere.

Product Hunt

Ryan Hoover had been an active blogger in product design, marketing, and startups. He had written over 150 essays, guest authored on dozens of blogs, and hosted brunches with company founders. Perhaps most importantly, he had also co-started an email newsletter called Startup Edition.[71] This gave him both a good-sized audience and connections to influential people within the technology sector.

It always bugged Hoover there wasn't a single place to find cool new products.[72] Techcrunch offered company news and HackerNews covered technology, but there was nowhere to go to find the latest cool new products launched each week.

In November 2013, Hoover created a simple mailing list to share the best new products he had discovered and invited a few dozen of his friends (an impressive group of founders, investors, and startup employees) to join.[73] Anybody subscribed to Hoover's Product Hunt list could add the best products they had seen. Each day a digest was sent to all members. By the end of the first week over 400 people had subscribed, and Hoover realized he was on to something big[74].

Hoover was naturally familiar with social news aggregators such as Reddit and HackerNews. Perhaps something similar could be created for products? Instead of members sharing the latest tech news, they would share the cool products they had heard about. Hoover shared the idea with his buddy Nathan Bashaw, who volunteered to code the site over Thanksgiving. On Dec 4, 2013, Product Hunt went live.

---

71 https://medium.com/@rrhoover/
    building-a-startup-build-an-audience-first-9fbba4f1fa15
72 https://www.fastcompany.com/3024472/
    how-we-got-our-first-2000-users-doing-things-that-dont-scale
73 https://www.groovehq.com/blog/ryan-hoover-product-hunt
74 https://thenextweb.com/insider/2017/05/04/
    product-hunt-story-began-according-founder-ryan-hoover/

By the end of the first day, the community had grown from 100 to 400 members. Just under three weeks later, with a small promotional push and a lot of direct outreach to members, the community had over 2,000 members. Each early contributor was asked to do one of two simple things: *share a product* or *share an article.*

Product Hunt had two major assets. First, almost anyone can share links. Most people do it every day already. It takes just a few seconds and is fun to do. Whereas sharing tips in a community takes expertise, it's simply a member's way of saying *"Hey, I found this interesting, you might too!".*

Second, Product Hunt made it as simple as possible for members to share links. Sure, this can happen in a forum, but as Aggiato and the team at Vorwerk learned, forums aren't well designed for anything beyond questions and answers. Links don't show up well, it's not the expected behavior, and posters are expected to write a lot of text too. To share links on forums, members almost have to go *against* the expected behavior. On ProductHunt, members fill in a few details and they're done. Better yet, they're simply doing what others are already doing.

Within a few years the community had reached 1m+ users and began to expand beyond technology. Fashion Hunt, for example, highlights the best new products in fashion. Long-term, Hoover hopes to be the home to communities for fashion, games, movies, music, and more[75] [76]

Even for organizations that can't copy Product Hunt directly, asking members to not only share expertise but also useful links broadens the number of potential participants beyond the extreme few.

In December 2016, the community was acquired by AngelList for $20m. Shortly after the deal was announced, Hoover stated: *"AngelList is not buying Product Hunt to start monetizing, it's*

---

75   http://mashable.com/2014/10/11/ryan-hoover-product-hunt/

76   To further prove the point about branching out to multiple streams of value, ProductHunt launched a feature to *ask the community* for product ideas in April 2017.

to help build the community". Naturally, the community was invited to a huge party in January to celebrate the acquisition[77].

Thus far, all of the contributions we've seen (sharing resources, solutions, tips, and links) contribute to a direct end goal. They save money on customer support, make customers and employees more successful, and make people smarter. But there is one other way members can support the community: by sharing effort.

Ben's Friends

At the age of 29, Ben Munoz had a brain aneurysm.

The aneurysm was caused by a rare disease he had never heard of: *Arteriovenous Malformations (AVM)*.[78] AVM is an abnormal formation of blood vessels that increases the likelihood of bleeding. If the bleeding occurs in the body, it can be hazardous; if it occurs in the brain, it is often fatal. In Munoz's case, it led to a stroke and years of radiotherapy, neurosurgery, and other treatments.

Munoz soon discovered an additional complication from having a rare disease. He could find plenty of medical information online and talk to doctors about the physiological aspects of the disease, but for the *psychological* aspects of the disease, he was at a loss:

> *"There wasn't really anyone I could really connect to,"* Munoz explains. *"To ask how was it? What was the treatment like? What are you going through? etcetera…"*

Munoz decided to launch his own community for AVM survivors (avmsurvivors.org) on a new platform called Ning. Ning offered two major benefits. First, it didn't require any technical expertise

---

77   https://thenextweb.com/insider/2017/05/04/
      product-hunt-story-began-according-founder-ryan-hoover/
78   https://www.forbes.com/sites/sarahmckinney/2014/03/01/
      this-29-year-old-had-a-brain-aneurism-you-wont-believe-what-he-
      did-next/#78ccd46b63b8

to create and run a community. Second, (perhaps most importantly for Munoz), it was free.[79]

To get started, Munoz asked friends to join and make the platform look busy:

> *"At first it was just 10 people, all friends of mine. None of them had AVM, they just wanted to support me."* Munoz continues: *"Then I broadcasted an announcement to the mailing list of Harvard Medical School, Department of Surgery and a few more joined. I asked people to share their stories and we now had content".*

By the end of the first month, Munoz had 100 people. This soon picked up to 200 and then to 300. As the community grew and matured, it began to attract larger levels of search traffic and word began to spread naturally. The community quick grew to thousands of members and an audience in the hundreds of thousands of visitors.

Munoz had proved that communities for rare diseases could not only work but could really help a lot of people. Working with Scott Orn, his Kellogg Business School friend, Munoz began repeating the concept for other diseases too. Within a few years, they had created a network of 30+ communities for rare diseases overlooked by other platforms.

Around this time, Munoz and Orn also made the remarkably noble decision not to turn this hard-built network into a business opportunity. They decided to forgo venture capital and instead become a non-profit organization under the name 'Ben's Friends'. This decision had two major consequences. First, it ensured every network would remain focused on members and untainted by a profit motive. There would never be any pressure to share information, sell advertising, or run focus groups. In the long-term, this might seem like a prescient decision. However, it also meant the future growth and success of the community

---

79 From 2006 to 2011, Ning was largely supported by advertising revenue. In 2011 it offered paid-only options. Still cheap compared to the market. Disclosure: We consulted with Ning for 18 months between 2013 and 2014 and advised Ben's Friends (to leave Ning) in 2015.

would be entirely dependent upon the goodwill (charity and time) of others. Even today, the entire network is a side-project for both Munoz and Orn, both of whom have day jobs.

As communities grow they require more time and resources. These resources cover the platform (web hosting, development etc...) and the people (who remove the bad stuff, promote the good stuff, ensure questions get good and accurate responses).

If *Ben's Friends* was going to survive, Munoz needed to get more members to give up more of their time to support the community. He began hunting people who might be great supporters and tempting them with the only thing he had to offer, *power.*

> "*If we notice members posting a lot and answering a ton of questions, we try to encourage that. Often we will invite them to become a 'greeter' within the community. Every single person that joins our network receives a personal welcome from one of our greeters. [...] If they prove themselves to be emotionally mature and empathetic, they get a different badge and are invited to become a moderator.*

Munoz relied upon his audience's need for competence and autonomy. The roles remained exclusive. Even with a limited budget, Munoz didn't need to persuade as many people as possible to become volunteers. He turned volunteerism into an act of pride and status (sometimes known as the *Tom Sawyer Effect*). Volunteering becomes a reward based upon a member's previous contributions.

Munoz's moderators, like the leaders in Chapter 3, have unique powers to remove spammers and approve new members. Moderators of each network also get access to a private forum where they can bond with each other and share ideas. This, in turn, encourages people to make more positive contributions to the community. But, Munoz adds, the unique access doesn't stop there:

> "*These privileges go all the way up to the highest moderator support level. Our top moderator is a retired surgeon in Montana and has full access to everything except for the DNS*

of the site. He can install plugins, update logos and banners, and change anything at the sysadmin root level."

This approach has allowed the network to grow to 35 sites with 50,000+ members and hundreds of thousands of unique visitors every single month. Amazingly, the entire project runs on a budget of less than $100k per year.

Members don't need to be experts to help the community. Almost every large community has volunteers, not just leaders, who give up their time to help moderate, remove bad content, and keep communities active and going. Volunteers can create and update content, share useful information, and keep the train on track if they're given the right appreciation and status. Most importantly, these volunteer roles create an emotional benefit members would struggle to get elsewhere, an *indispensable* feeling of doing good for others.

Summary

Almost every kind of community today needs members willing to educate others and support the community. However, members will only help educate and support the community if the rewards of the contribution are greater than the costs. One method of doing this is to boost the rewards with special status or having unique access.

Garrett at PMI enforced relentlessly high standards for any contributions to make the cut. An accepted contribution became a status symbol. Spotify created a unique reward program with access to the organization, special status within the community, and unique abilities. The other option is to reduce they're costs. It's a lot easier to get people to make contributions if they've asked to do the things they have the time, expertise, and motivation to do.

Providing multiple ways for people to contribute is key. This might mean asking for great resources, as Garrett did, but it's more likely to mean asking members to share a tip, answer a question, share link, or take a volunteer role in the community. The very community can be designed for this purpose.

Every member right now could be contributing more than they do today if they're asked (and nudged).

The book up to now has been devoted to getting members to make their best possible contribution to a community. We achieve this not by asking for less but asking for more. We motivate members by satisfying their need for instant gratification and then slowly helping them to feel more competent, a greater sense of autonomy, and a stronger relationship to other members (status). This can only happen when members are doing things that matter. It only happens when we turn members into ALLIES: people who advocate, lead, learn, provide insights, educate, and support the community.

The objective for anyone building a brand community is to get more from community members, not less. Help members make the best contribution they can make. Turn community members into ALLIES.

PART 2
TURN COLLEAGUES INTO ALLIES

Chapter 7

IDEALISTS FINISH LAST

"*I used to have a very purist view of community,*" says LinkedIn's Global Head of Community, Maria Ogneva. She continues with a self-reprimanding wince: "*I thought community, yay, everyone should be doing that. Bosses and executives should support it because it's a good thing for them to do.*"

The problem with being a purist, as Ogneva half-jokingly elaborates, is "*you spend much of your time keeping others from tainting the community with their evil, capitalist, motives.*"

Sitting in the canteen of LinkedIn's new ultramodern San Francisco Headquarters, in June 2017, Ogneva can reflect upon a community career that began promisingly, stalled, and then accelerated her to about as high as anyone in the community world can climb.

During those stalled years, Ogneva repeatedly found herself in an isolated silo wondering why her colleagues '*just didn't get it*'. She often found herself not moving towards the same goals as the rest of her organization.

The pattern repeated itself a few times before it dawned on Ogneva maybe the problem wasn't the businesses she was working for, it was her. *She was the problem.* She was so consumed with having a happy, vibrant, untainted community that she wasn't getting the support she needed to drive it forward:

> "*The community [of a former employer] could've been much more. It should've been able to help every member of the executive team get to what they were striving towards. But instead I didn't capture that opportunity.*"

What if, instead of trying to protect the community from her colleagues, she proactively engaged her colleagues in creating it? What if she aligned the goals of the community to the goals of her colleagues? What if she threw away the job description (often to drive engagement) and instead became more of a collaborator? This revelation, says Ogneva, changed everything:

> *"Today I don't just assume it's good to connect with customers. I check what it's actually doing for the company. I bring people with me even if it means moving a little slower than I want to. Because if I don't, I risk building something that's not relevant to, or supported by, the people I work with. So I go on the journey with them, listen to their concerns, address them, and figure out how they can become heroes through the community."*

Ogneva has discovered it can't be her alone doing this work. It has to be her boss and executives accepting and spreading the community successes. She has to keep the community in what she calls *"the regular flow"* of the business, useful in the day to day work with her colleagues. The more the community helps her colleagues, the more her colleagues support her in turn. It's this support that drives even further growth of the community.

Instead of sitting in a silo with dwindling resources, she has the resources to match her vision, and a career on a sharply upward trajectory.

In the San Francisco's Lower Mission district, Camilla,[80] a community manager at Yahoo, finds herself in a very different position:

"Things have changed a lot since we last spoke," Camilla begins somberly. That morning, June 13, 2017, Yahoo had revealed it had been acquired by Verizon for $4.56nn. This was good news for shareholders, bad news for employees. Verizon announced they would be cutting 15% of Yahoo's staff.

> *"Other people tell me the signs. Weird notices are put up at meeting rooms. Double packets of Kleenex tissues are placed in each room. We know it's coming to our department."*

---

80   *Not her real name.*

Camilla is in the firing line because she's not directly employed by Yahoo. A contractor via a third party, her contract (which is typically renewed without fuss) had just seven days remaining. Her boss couldn't tell her whether her contract would be renewed. He wasn't being evasive; he didn't know if he would be there after the merger let alone in a position to renew anyone's contract.

In the gig economy, even engagement can be contracted 'as needed'. Camilla discovered that need can vanish suddenly. When the value of engagement is called into question, which happens often during major internal changes, outside contractors are the easiest to let go. Camilla was upset, but surprisingly understanding of the decision:

> "Everyone in sales is fine, those guys all make money. [...] If I was a new manager, I'd probably cut the community team too. We don't make money."

Not all brand communities need to directly drive money. Some generate great ideas that help develop better products and solve problems. But communities that don't directly drive money need *widespread support* to survive...especially from departments they're trying to help. Camilla didn't have this support, and the product team was the worst:

> "The product team ignores us. They think we're just some small little thing. They don't see what the value would be from the community."

Camilla truly loves her work and the job. By her own account, she has done almost everything her job required of her. She's taken training and delivered great increases in engagement. Her boss is on her side too:

> "I've created strategies, managed teams, and managed to show results of what we're doing. It's the first job where I truly felt like I was growing and had the support to do amazing things."

Camilla is a purist. She's one of many people building brand communities who love the work and excel at driving engagement.

They do everything they're told to do but still find themselves at the bottom of the career ladder, with few resources, and limited respect. A few, like Camilla, suddenly find themselves out of work entirely.

The biggest difference between Ogneva and Camilla isn't their age, their skillset, or even the companies they work for. Both have large communities. The biggest difference is how they approach their work.

When Ogneva describes her work, she talks about the relationships she's building internally and the never ending struggle to prove the value of what she does to get more executives across the organization involved. Her colleagues might not support her yet, but they will in time.

When Camilla talks about her work she mentions the members she's gotten to know, the activities she's initiated in the community, and the processes for removing bad comments and keeping things on track. She talks about the engagement metrics going up and how much better she's become at engaging members.

Where Ogneva described how she was winning over skeptical colleagues, Camilla describes such skepticism as static fact of life (*"The product team ignore us"*). To Camilla, this was simply the way things were. She will keep doing everything she can to get as much engagement as possible and leave the product team to their own devices. As long as she keeps her head down, delights her members, and her boss likes her *she will be fine.*

Ogneva puts the needs of the business and the people she works with first. Her community is about clear business results. Camilla puts the needs of her members first. She finds out what members want to do and does more of it. If her colleagues don't get why having a happy community is important, that's their problem. Only today it isn't. Today it's very much Camilla's problem.

Like many others, Camilla hasn't confronted the limitations of just being the community person yet. This is the reason she's on the lowest rungs of the community ladder without great career prospects. It's the reason she and her team haven't gained more resources. It's the reason the product team *didn't get it*. She doesn't command the respect and authority to win other people over because she hasn't made the psychological switch to realize *it's her responsibility to win them over*.

Camilla isn't alone. Hundreds of thousands of social media, online engagement, and online community professionals around the world have discovered it's a lot easier to engage members in the community than to talk to their colleagues about the community. It's a lot more exciting to keep growing engagement than engage their skeptical colleagues.

Being a purist means believing in the innate *goodness* of building a community—even the word *'community'* tingles with noble, purist ideals. Yet it's these very same purist ideals that eventually hold the community back. In the business world, purist community beliefs are naive at best and disruptive at worst. This pegs Camilla and thousands of her peers as the *'online engagement person'*. They are the people whose job it is to talk people online instead of building a truly *indispensable community*.

Building an indispensable community requires a change in mindset from a *'hands off my community'* purist to a *'what would you like to see from the community?'* realist. It requires a set of skills purists dismiss, such as building internal relationships, measuring results, and communicating success persuasively. It requires recognizing that the business is paying for the community and its bottom line wants clear results. A community can't be only a place for members to hang out and chat about a topic. It has to be a place to get members to make incredible contributions that help the business.

Building an indispensable community means your mission is to get support and win people over. It's never the boss *'who doesn't get it'*, it's the community team who hasn't yet understood what the boss needs or helped explain what she needs. Sometimes, it's a case of acquiescence. The community team was tasked to drive engagement and never questioned whether that was the most effective assignment.

The entire success of a community depends upon winning over colleagues and making sure the community is delivering results. No one is going to miraculously appreciate the value of people talking to each other on the internet just because the number of conversations is really, really, high. High engagement didn't help Ogneva and didn't save Camilla. The only thing that *does* help is showing an incredible impact upon what colleagues care about: like leads generated, costs saved, results improved, etc...

Chapter 8

THE ENGAGEMENT TRAP

Since 1979, Carnival Cruise Lines has built a popular brand offering fun, cheap, and less stuffy, Las Vegas-themed cruises throughout the Caribbean. A typical day on one of its 25 *'Fun Ships'* involves sunbathing, casinos, shopping, massages, games, and shows. In 2010, Carnival noticed passengers wanted help planning their trips and keeping in touch with friends. So they launched a new community, *FunVille*[81].

FunVille was an instant success. Most activity in FunVille was lighthearted, a place for members to casually chat with one another and enjoy themselves. The prevailing logic was the more people visited and stayed in the community, the better it would be for Carnival.

In six years, tens of thousands of members had published over 1.6 million posts. Posts were advice about future cruises or members playing games and having fun. The community was the very epitome of what most brands want: thousands of passionate fans having a lot of fun. The fun ended on June 9, 2016, when Carnival closed FunVille for good.

It didn't make any sense. Why would a successful company suddenly decide to close such an active, popular community? Even the staff didn't get it. As one former community manager complained:

> *"I really don't understand letting it go, we're the only cruise line that offers one [community] [...] it still gets traffic that most companies would kill for."*

---

81   https://www.bizjournals.com/southflorida/blog/cruise_industry_
      report/2010/01/carnival_launches_online_funville.html

It's one thing for a company to close down a ghost town, a community with almost no activity. It's another thing entirely to get rid of an active community with thousands of members and millions of posts. Wouldn't closing a community mean furious customers flee to competitors, a sudden collapse in web traffic, and the death of innovation? The answer is no. A year later, despite the customer resentment and furor, Carnival posted record profits.[82]

In 2016, Seattle software company, Moz, later, released most of their community team. A few months later they announced they had finally returned to profit. Airbnb downsized most of their community team, yet still the company thrives. How can this be happening if brand communities are as valuable as we believe them to be?

In 2009, the *Harvard Business Review* published the famous story of the Harley Davidson Owners' Group. In the early 1980s, the struggling motorcycle company built a powerful network of Harley Davidson Owners across the USA. This turned the company from the brink of bankruptcy into a company worth $7.8bn[83].

Stories like this provide the raison d'etre for building a community. It's why we need to turn our customers into a community and why we want the members of our communities to be as engaged as possible. But the Harley example hides a more nuanced truth.

Although Harley Davidson sales did rise after launching the Harley Davidson Ownership Group, that's just one part of a far bigger story. Harley Davidson also persuaded the US government to slap a massive 49.4% import tariff on better Japanese bikes,[84] increased the number of bikes without defects from a shockingly low 50% to an impressive 98%, and aggressively repositioned

---

82   https://www.statista.com/statistics/266272/
      revenue-of-cruise-operator-carnival-corporation-und-plc/
83   https://hbr.org/2009/04/getting-brand-communities-right
84   http://archive.fortune.com/magazines/fortune/fortune_
      archive/1989/09/25/72503/index.htm

the brand to target a new group of consumers.[85] Did the Harley Davidson Owner Group help? Yes, most probably[86]. But it was one piece of a much bigger puzzle.

Another example is Dell. As we've seen, from the mid-00s to the early 2010s, Dell was winning awards for its online engagement, social media, and community building efforts. At the same time its revenues tanked, the share price plunged, and the company became a second-rate equipment manufacturer. A former Dell staffer described this problem: *"That's what happens when Apple starts releasing better laptops."* Where's the community loyalty if customers immediately leap to the next product?

Stories like Harley Davidson and Dell are used to justify building a brand community, often with the benefits exaggerated and the costs downplayed. Studies may show incredible theoretical benefits but an accountant can't see them on the balance sheet.

Community Members Always Buy More

In 2009, Syncapse (a now-defunct social media marketing agency) published a report suggesting a Facebook fan was worth $71.84.[87] [88] If this were true, it would mean Facebook had caused an explosion in sales across the globe. It would make the 107m+ Coca-Cola fan page members worth $7.7bn dollars.

Now, it's certainly possible Coca Cola has seen an explosion in sales since launching their fan page.[89] Perhaps 107 million fans each buy $71.84 more Coca Cola after seeing updates in their Facebook feed. But it's unlikely. The more feasible explanation is that the study is bogus.

The problem with using *"members buy/do [x] more than non members..."* is it creates a world with inflated theoretical

---

85   https://www.scribd.com/document/241135265/
Forbes-The-Turnaround-at-Harley-Davidson

86   We were unable to find any study of the group's impact itself.

87   Syncapse went bankrupt in 2013, owing millions of dollars in debt.

88   www.i-marketing-net.com/wp-content/uploads-neu/syncapse-value-of-a-facebook-fan.pdf

89   Gross sales revenue has dropped since 2012.

benefits that don't show up in practice. Ten thousand members might spend $100 more than non-members, but the CFO isn't seeing that extra $1,000,000 show up in the balance sheet. As Allison Leahy mentioned, it's this kind of statistic *"community managers love to share, but CFOs will knock down every time and analysts will question."* This is classic *selection bias.*

For example, imagine Apple launched a brand new community for customers to ask questions. Clearly, the more Apple products a customer owns, the more likely one will break and they will go to the community to seek help. A study of Apple community members will inevitably find they buy more products than non-members. In statistics, this is known as correlation.

Nothing is wrong with correlation. Correlation establishes a possible relationship between two or more variables; i.e. being a community member (variable 1) and the number of Apple products purchased (variable 2). The problem is when correlation is confused with *causation.*

It's easy to study this data and declare: *"customers in our community purchase 200% more than non-members."*[90] While this is true, it's false to say it's caused by the community. The reverse is equally (if not more) plausible. *Customers who purchase 200% more are 200% more likely to join the community.*[91] Remember: people who join a brand community already like the brand, and for the most part, are already the best customers. Correlations are easy to find but, like Facebook fans, aren't worth much. Eventually, the CEO is going to notice the supposed benefits of the community aren't translating into better bottom line. The community starts to look like an unnecessary extravagance.

It's not just communities for paying customers that fall into this trap. Most brand communities do too. Are employees who participate in the community more productive or are productive employees more likely to join the community? Do people quit smoking as a result of a non-smoking community or does the

---

90   https://cmxhub.com/article/erica-kuhl-salesforce-community-roi/
91   Usually the answer is somewhere between the two. The community may have increased purchases a little but those more likely to buy were also more likely to join the community.

community attract people more likely to quit smoking? Does joining the community increase someone's odds of buying or do likely customers join the community? Does the community increase the expertise of members or are experts more likely to join the community? It's hard to separate the cause from the effect.

These aren't the howls of amateur statistics geeks but a fundamental question about building a brand community. If mere engagement alone drives results, community managers should do *everything in their power to drive as much engagement as possible*. This leads them straight into *the engagement trap*.

The Engagement Trap

The engagement trap begins when the community is measured by the amount of engagement (or activity) it creates—the number of active members, posts, contributions, likes, shares, retweets, etc… It doesn't take long to realise the best way to increase engagement is to lower the bar for participation. Asking members to make the simplest possible contribution that can be measured, such as asking for clicks over comments, simple jokes over sharing expertise, and off-topic discussions over soliciting valuable feedback, is common practice.

Once a community begins to fall down the ladder of valuable contributions, it's very hard to climb back up. Persuading members used to joking around to spend a few hours a week sharing their best expertise is difficult and would lead to an instant drop in engagement, the very thing on which the community manager is measured. Once engagement metrics are the goal, it's logical to pursue the actions that drive the most engagement. But the best results come from better, not more, contributions.

Anyone whose job is measured by engagement metrics is caught in the engagement trap. Everyone who begins the day replying to discussions, creating content to get views, and trying to get more people to join and participate is usually caught in the trap.

In November 2015, Lindsay Starke sat in Higher Logic's office, on the outskirts of Washington, DC, contemplating what to do. Higher Logic provides a platform for associations to create communities for their members. Starke's job was to ensure these communities were successful.

The association sector is a huge industry, which ranges from mega-associations like the American Association for Retired Persons (AARP), with billion dollar budgets, all the way down to tiny outfits like the Association for the Preservation of the Coelacanth.[92]

One client, an association of engineers, wanted her to create content based on the field's most popular topics (autonomous vehicles and electric cars). But she felt increasingly uneasy about the content strategy her client had asked her to execute.

Starke wasn't a newcomer to associations. She had cut her community teeth helping build the Loop, a community for the *Professional Photographers of America*. But she wasn't an engineering expert. Could she really tell her client she knew what their members needed to do better than they did?

Still, she began chasing engagement. It was a big mistake, as Starke explains:

> "*I was a dum dum [...] Because I wasn't an SME [subject matter expert], I went with their content strategy, and I tried to spur lots of discussions around the flavor of the week.*"

At first, things went well. The engagement metrics rose and the client was happy. Over the next few months, it became harder to find buzzy topics to drive activity and participation dwindled. The client wanted answers and Starke didn't have any. She began researching the history of organic posts and, crucially, interviewing members of the community. This soon led her to a forehead-slapping realization:

> "*I eventually realized that they [the members] didn't want a place to discuss the relative merits of a car that can be hacked or fly or whatever the big deal was.*"

Association members aren't paying dues to be kept engaged or entertained. They're paying their dues (in part) to have access

---

92 A rare order of fish, apparently.

to a community that helps them solve their daily engineering problems. Starke wasn't building an *indispensable community* members couldn't afford to live without, she was building a community that was briefly amusing but completely dispensable. Popular topics can attract momentary attention, but real engagement and results would come only if members couldn't afford to lose to the community. This insight shifted the conversation from "*Do you think we will ever have autonomous, electric cars?*" towards detailed questions like: "*I want some insight on a proper and accurate way of testing LIN bus communications problems between master-slave components. I'm not sure if the line voltage is a good indicator of any potential issues. An oscilloscope works better but I still can't determine if there is a communication problem and how to spot it.*"

The goalposts shifted from chasing lots of engagement to getting members to ask questions and finding actionable answers. The community became indispensable to members. Why would anyone cancel their membership if they could rely upon getting a quick answer to their toughest problems from an army of experts? It's obvious in hindsight, but tricky to see in foresight. Especially when the pressure is on from clients and executives to boost engagement.

It's not enough to believe communities are about more than driving engagement; colleagues, clients, peers, vendors, and others need to believe it too. Far too many people value a community by the level of activity it creates. They pressure others to use the same benchmarks for success. Driving a lot of engagement is pointless unless it's also delivering indispensable information. The only way to resist the pressure of chasing engagement is to shows it's not the quantity of engagement that matters, but what comes from that engagement. But how? Simple tools to measure the real value of engagement don't exist.

Google Analytics

In August 2004, David Frieberg and Wesley Chang, two Google executives, went shopping for a web analytics firm at the Search Engine Strategies Conference. Their goal was to solve one of

Google's most pressing problems, *measuring the value of digital advertising.*

Their fiercest competitor, Yahoo, had recently acquired Overture (and its Keylime search marketing tool) for $1.63bn. The pressure was on to come up with a better tool or lose advertisers.

At the conference, David and Wesley made contact with Urchin, a growing web analytics business. Urchin began as WebDepot, a web development firm, in the mid-90s, creating websites for clients and charging them for hosting.[93] To calculate hosting costs, they created a log analyzer with an attractive user interface.[94] It took a few years, but the team soon realized licensing the tool to analyze web traffic was more profitable than creating the sites themselves. Urchin stopped making websites and instead signed a couple of major deals with ISP providers. Urchin soon became one of the web's most popular web analytics companies.[95] [96]

By April 2005, Google concluded a deal to acquire Urchin, for $30m in stock, and re-released it as Google Analytics seven frantic months later. Google Analytics was an instant hit. Approximately 100,000 accounts were created within the first week.[97] Today, Google Analytics measures the success of 50m+ sites and has captured a whopping 83.5% share of the web analytics market.[98]

In a single swoop, Google Analytics solved one of the company's biggest challenges. Since Google Analytics is mostly free, no one

---

93   http://jacobsschool.ucsd.edu/pulse/summer2005/alumni.shtml

94   Every web server has logs showing which IP addresses downloaded which pages.

95   http://www.attendly.com/
the-real-story-on-how-google-analytics-got-started/

96   https://www.stonetemple.com/
interview-of-google-analytics-brett-crosby/

97   https://brianclifton.com/blog/2015/11/10/
google-analytics-is-10-what-has-changed/

98   Google doesn't publish metrics; these are taken from various surveys and analysis which vary considerably. https://w3techs.com/
technologies/overview/traffic_analysis/all

needs buying approval to use it.[99] And it's so simple, almost anyone can add Google Analytics to their site by inserting a single line of javascript into the <header> tab of the main page. Each time the page loads for a visitor, Google uploads the data to their analytics server and presents the aggregated information in easy to understand graphics.

These are tools designed to measure advertising, not communities. Advertisers care about engagement, not changes in behavior. More engagement equals more advertising revenue. Communities need to measure changes in behavior and Google Analytics can't reveal what individual members are doing. It's very difficult to answer questions like:[100]

- How many community members are advocating and attracting new customers?
- Are members buying more as a result of the community?
- Are members generating useful product ideas which have been implemented?
- Are members identifying themselves as useful leads for the sales team?
- Are members sharing useful knowledge with one another that save time?

Google Analytics essentially *democratized analytics.* Analytics went from being the domain of the expert to the purview of the amateur. Anyone could now easily gather, analyze, and present data. Instead of measuring the behavior that matters, brands track the easiest behavior to measure. It's very hard to escape the engagement trap without this data. No other easy metrics can be applied.

Once a community is measured by the easiest metrics to collect, it becomes trapped by them. Data can be dressed in attractive ways, but it's always a victim of the same problem.

---

99   There is a premium version of Google Analytics for business.
100 There are increasingly some tools that enable this kind of data. But they're not yet widely used. Those that are also face their own data protection challenges.

The metrics used to prove the value of the community are metrics that don't help colleagues within the business. If you've ever gone into a meeting to report on the level of engagement, you're caught in the engagement trap. You will remain there forever, struggling to justify the value of the community, until Judgement Day arrives.

RealSelf and Judgement Day

When an upper management executive questions whether the value of engagement is really worth the cost, it's Judgement Day. If engagement can't be linked to concrete results, why should an organization continue to invest in engagement?

The biggest trigger of Judgement Day is a sudden change. At Moz, an unexpected business downturn led to a community team being reduced from ten to two people. Executive changes might also precipitate Judgement Day. Often, a new CFO or senior executive will take a hard look at any spending that isn't clearly driving outcomes and make cuts in the community team (as was the case at Airbnb).

Most commonly, it coincides with a growing realization that the community approach may not be the most effective method for a business to achieve its strategy. For example, in 2017, RealSelf CEO Tom Seery realized his company was a market-place, not an advertising platform.

Seery founded RealSelf in 2006, after his wife, Krista, struggled to find information about a $2,000 laser skin treatment. Krista was perplexed she *couldn't get the same kind of quality infor-mation about laser procedures as she could about a hotel's towels or its spa facilities.*[101] At the time, reviews were available, but they were scattered in anonymous, hard to-reach-corners of the web. RealSelf's mission was to bring transparency to an opaque industry. It was the perfect market: a $10bn industry set for big growth as the richest generation in American history

---

101 https://www.entrepreneur.com/article/217351

retired. This market had also been almost entirely ignored by the squeamish middle-aged investors of Silicon Valley.

The RealSelf model is simple. Doctors pay a fee to have their elective surgery practice listed next to relevant results and reviews on RealSelf. The doctors, in return, get good quality leads and the audience gets more information to help them make an informed decision. The early years were focused on aggregating in-depth, unique insights and facts that are hard to find elsewhere. As Seery once noted, this wasn't "*just a bunch of editors the company has hired,*"[102] it was real people sharing real concerns and real results (hence the name, *RealSelf*).

As the company grew, however, the model of users answering each others' medical questions became a ticking legal timebomb. So RealSelf created a section where doctors answered moderated questions from people considering elective surgery. The community effort now focused on two areas from people on the site who had elective surgery. The first was getting the reviews and experiences from people whom have had elective surgery on the site. The second was a questions and answers area where members could get expert advice from doctors.

As engagement grew, a small team of six staff (two on site, four remote) were hired to manage the community. Their mission was to engage people, persuade them to submit reviews, and foster discussions that would encourage people to take elective procedures. In the words of one former community manager, having members engage and feel safe would get more people to *decide* to have surgery in the first place:

> "*[...] the decision to have these procedures is a deeply emotional one, And we know—though we can't quantify it—that folks thinking about having a procedure at all would read those stories, get comfortable with the idea, and decide to find a doctor.*"

---

102 https://pando.com/2013/01/23/
      realself-makes-plastic-surgery-transparent/

The problem was the community team didn't have the data to back up their assumption. It's easy to fall victim to a success bias, confuse correlation with causation, and exaggerate the possible impact of the community. Does the community cause people to take elective surgery or does taking elective surgery cause people to participate in the community? Seery reflected on this problem too:

> *"We found that the way the community oriented was more for those people who had been through it and done it, not for people upfront who were trying to make that decision."*

In short, people don't go into a marketplace without already having made a decision to buy. Once someone has loaded Airbnb, Uber, or Upwork on their phone, they've already decided they need a place to stay, a car, or a freelancer. Seery believed the same was true of RealSelf. By the time someone had reached the site, they had already made a decision to have elective surgery. They didn't need a community to help them further along that process. As Seery noted, reading posts on a community can actually push members *"back up the [sales] funnel."*

The community team was looking at the top of the funnel ('*what gets people to decide to take elective surgery?*'). Seery, the CEO, was looking at results at the bottom of the funnel ('*what gets people who have decided to have elective surgery to contact a doctor?*'). As the ex-staffer explained, even if the community team's assumption was accurate, they didn't have the data to back it up.

> *"Tom's reasoning was the content being shared by the community was about the emotional experience of surgery and not so much whether the doctor they used was any good. So it didn't fit the conversion funnel well. [...] all we could argue was that the user generated content was what made people comfortable enough to convert."*

In 2017, RealSelf went through a transformational shift after a rebranding exercise, to become less of a platform to collect and pass on leads to doctors and more of a marketplace. The term 'marketplace' is key. A marketplace is focused upon conversions, not conversations. Airbnb, Upwork, or Uber users aren't personally greeted by a community professional and asked to participate in discussions. Instead, they're nudged to make a purchase and leave a review.

The shift to conversions left the community team adrift. They were focusing on the wrong goals at the wrong time. As the community manager noted: *"The problem was the executive team became obsessed about conversions at the expense of the community."*

Judgement Day befalls most members of a brand community team just when they're at their most comfortable, feeling most supported, and are working hard to drive their highest levels of engagement. The endless quest to get more people participating (RealSelf staff spend a lot of time sending direct messages to newcomers to nudge them to participate) came at the expense of determining how best to position the community to achieve the company's goals.

It's clear RealSelf executives wanted conversions and the community team knew that. Yet they continued to focus on *proving* the value of what they were already doing rather than *changing* what they were doing to get the necessary results. Instead of making the executive team's goals their own, they remained committed to what they had been doing for a decade (without being able to show results).

Sentimental feel good associations with a community notwithstanding, it's obvious Seery made the right move. If it's impossible to see whether community drives value, it makes sense to spend less on the community and more on activities which directly drive sales. Even the community manager agreed:

> *"Tom's perspective IS fairly reasonable—we did the same things for 10+ years, and he wasn't seeing definitively that it was working."*

It's impossible to build an indispensable community unless the community is directly aligned with the needs of executives. Communities that drive the maximum levels of engagement don't do that. Too many are built upon shaky assumptions. Very questionable data is often accepted as definitive proof of the community's value or the raison d'etre behind trying to get the engagement metrics up. The solution is for the community team members to challenge their own assumptions, answer their own worst criticisms, and figure out what outcomes senior executives need to see.

If the executive team *"suddenly becomes obsessed"* about conversions, the community needs to become obsessed about conversions too. They need to do this before their value is questioned. Because, by the time the value of community is brought into question, it's probably too late.

Summary

Engagement isn't bad; *chasing engagement is bad.*

A lot of engagement is a natural outcome of building an indispensable community. If members can't live without the community, they want to visit and participate every day. This naturally drives a lot of engagement. The danger is mistaking the symptom of successful engagement with the goal of building a community. No one measures the success of athletes by how hard they sweat. Once members are asked to make the easiest possible contributions, it becomes very difficult to build a community an organization finds indispensable. It's a classic engagement trap.

Executives need to see more engagement because that's the only viable metric of measuring the community. Yet the actions that drive the most engagement and those that build an indispensable community are completely different. It's hard to focus on outcomes when people expect the engagement metrics to go up. Eventually, the value of engagement will be called into question and the community team will face its Judgement Day. Judgement Day usually ends with the summary execution of the community team.

To escape the engagement trap, the community needs to show results the brand cares about. But the most popular measurement tools today are designed to track advertising metrics (clicks, likes, shares etc…) and not the long-term impact of behavior. Without better metrics, the community team will always struggle to resist the pressure from colleagues to show engagement metrics. Getting the right metrics needs to be a project with as much priority as getting the right behavior from members.

The only thing worse than Judgement Day is *never facing Judgement Day*. Without a Judgement Day, community teams can (and do) endlessly waste their company's resources, their community's potential, and their careers, getting people to click, like, and share content. Community teams can spend years struggling to get more resources, credibility, and respect.

Wouldn't it be better to challenge any activity designed solely for activity's sake? Wouldn't it feel better to make the community invaluable to colleagues and build powerful alliances throughout the company? Wouldn't it be incredible to finally get the resources to make the community truly indispensable?

Chapter 9

BECOME INDISPENSABLE

In 2016, a major multinational IT company asked FeverBee to calculate its community's value. In the 14 years since the community had been created for a small group of developers, it had expanded to other types of customers, languages, and interests. Now it's a behemoth any brand would be thrilled to host.

behemoths cost money, however... rather a lot of money! The community, now managed by a team of 10 professionals, incurs heavy technology costs, and even picks up the tab for events hosted around the world. For a long time, questioning the value of its members was unthinkable. Everyone simply knew having a thriving community filled with enthusiastic customers was incredibly valuable. The community had a multi-million dollar per year budget and eventually a senior executive asked why. Our staff interviews revealed a disconcerting truth: it wasn't only the executives who didn't understand the community's value; the staff managing the community didn't know either. A few named a range of benefits, but they weren't measuring them. That was *'someone else's job'*. Everyone agreed it would be crazy to shut the community down, or reduce its budget, but no one could explain why. The data hadn't been collected, let alone analyzed.

Far too many brand communities today exist to exist. They engage people to show engagement. At some point, someone thought it was a good idea to start a community. They weren't guided by any clear, specific, targets to hit. They certainly weren't headed towards an indispensable goal. And *indispensable is what matters.*

Members become ALLIES when they perform behaviors that matter. Plenty of activities members *can* perform are incredibly valuable. But unless a community has meaningful goals, it's impossible to know which behaviors matter. You can't hit a target that doesn't exist.

Increase Revenue	Reduce Costs
• **Increase retention rates** (customer loyalty, improving customer satisfaction/sentiment, reducing churn) • **Increase share of wallet** (average order value, frequency of purchase, upselling/downselling/cross-selling) • **Advertising revenue** (delivering more ads, higher advertising rates) • **Lead generation** (lead identification, customer advocacy, net promoter score, search engine traffic, reach/mentions) • **Lead conversion** (reduce lead conversion time, improve lead to visit conversion rates, improve lead to customer conversion rates) • **Develop better products** (idea generation, idea validation, identify bugs, improved speed to resolve problems)	• **Reduce customer service costs** (call deflection, indirect call deflection, improved first-contact resolution, decrease in average handling time) • **Reduce customer acquisition costs** (increase web traffic, lead generation, lead identification) • **Reduce research costs** (Focus groups, surveys, interviews) • **Reduce recruitment costs** (costs per applicant, cost per qualifying applicants, time-to-full productivity) • **Improve collaboration** (reduced time looking for information, higher productivity)
Help the organization achieve its goals (non-profit)	
• **Collective action** (peer-to-peer fundraising, donations, signatures) • **Social proof** • **Knowledge sharing**	

Working without goals is a curse for a community team, the results are limited respect, support, and influence. The team can suddenly find itself out of work, the community effort abandoned. Everyone building a brand community should have goals, to be able to say, "*This is what I've achieved...this is why the community exists!... this is why I deserve more support!*"

Goals shouldn't be vague or removed from metrics that matter to the business. Yes, engagement can influence loyalty and loyalty can influence whether customers stay or go. But that's two layers removed from value. Other factors such as price, quality, customer support, and level of competition also influence loyalty. It's hard to prove the community made the difference.

Both the RealSelf CEO and the community team wanted the community to attract new customers for their clients (surgeons). But the community team focused on the top of the funnel (helping people feel comfortable to make the decision to have surgery), while the CEO focused on the bottom of the funnel (getting people to decide which surgeon to pick). The community team was focused on several layers removed from value, while the CEO was focused on immediate value.

Goals connect the brand community to the areas where it can most clearly increase revenue, reduce costs, or, in the case of non-profits, help the organization best achieve its mission. A brand community can help in plenty of ways; the most common are in the table above.[103]

If a brand community doesn't directly connect to one of the above goals, there is usually a problem.

Swiftkey

Swiftkey is a predictive input technology that makes typing on a phone easier through a combination of artificial learning and predicting the next word before it's typed. The company was founded in 2010, raised $17.5m in fundraising in 2013, and was acquired by Microsoft, for $250m, in 2016. It's a classic, if low key, Silicon Valley success story.

Upon acquiring one of the most popular (and profitable) paid apps in the world, Microsoft took the unusual step of releasing it for free. This had two advantages. First, it increased sales of custom themes (which were more profitable than the app). Second, it allowed the app to enter new markets, like India and

---

103 Adapted from www.FeverBee.com/roi

China, that had been tough to crack. Making the app free was a mixed blessing for the community team. On the one hand, it removed the pressure to prove it was directly generating revenue, but on the other hand it raised the question of why should SwiftKey need a community at all?

While the CEO, CMO, and CTO were supportive of the community, no one had yet figured out how to get much value from it. Eric Shaw and Ryan Paredez, who arrived at Microsoft through its acquisition of SwiftKey, knew early on their members *really* wanted to try new versions of the product. They focused their community efforts on putting pre-beta material (early designs, prototypes, sketches, and surveys) in their members' hands as soon as possible. The purpose of the community, they determined, would be to gather useful feedback for engineers. But product feedback only has value if engineers use it and they weren't.

This is the danger of selecting possible goals from a random list. The community can drive results no one cares about. It's dangerous to set a big noble goal everyone supports in theory but that no one is on the hook for achieving. Few people truly care about these goals. As Maria Ogneva said, *"There is no point trying to fix something the organization doesn't want to fix."* Or to put it even better, *"There is no point trying to fix something someone specific within the organization doesn't want to fix."*

SwiftKey's product engineers wanted to create the best products possible, but they were already getting plenty of ideas, feature requests, and bug reports to work with through other customer support channels. Having an additional source of feedback wasn't a priority.

Mitt Romney was wrong when he said *"corporations are people."* They're not, but they are made up of people. People have hopes, fears, and complex motivations. Each person has his or her own unique goals and needs. It's not a good idea to set a goal for a community without finding out *specifically* what colleagues need first. Shaw knew if the feedback was ever going to be used, he needed to learn more about his engineers. He began by attending engineering team meetings. He soon discovered the problem:

"I learned there was a pretty big gap between our feedback and engineering cycles. Giving engineering the right feedback at the wrong time doesn't help. So I made it my crusade to be in every meeting and make sure that people from our team got invited to every sprint planning session [period of intense development]."

Feedback that arrived during an engineering sprint wasn't anywhere near as useful as feedback that arrived when decisions were being made about what to pursue next. This is obvious enough in hindsight but surprisingly hard to appreciate in foresight. Shaw and Paredez may never have discovered this lesson without attending the meetings of other teams.

Shaw's next step was to use his insight to start building processes for team leads, project managers, and others to use the community at every level in their decision making. It wasn't enough to be aware of the community; his colleagues needed to know how to use it. This meant being proactive about providing value.

Every two months, Paredez publishes a survey to a randomly selected group of community members asking the same questions. He asks other teams if they have any questions they want to include in the survey—about an existing feature, design, or anything that could be useful. Even no response can be useful: *"It suggests there's nothing wrong."*

Paredez and Shaw are a great example of taking the time to understand exactly what engineering needed (and when!) and then delivering on that need. This doesn't just yield more value to SwiftKey, it yields more value to members, too. Instead of trying to create content to get people to participate in discussions, they provide members with a meaningful opportunity to influence the product they love.

They're slowly making their community indispensable to engineering, but first they had to make themselves visible and know *specifically* what others needed. According to Shaw, attending their meetings helped build an understanding of what engineers needed, when they needed it, and made the community team visible: *"I made sure the teams that were out there knew the kinds of things we were doing, saw the impact we were trying to achieve and knew we were a resource for them. A lot of it was about discoverability of the team and getting an understanding of what they did [...] You can't be reactive. You have to go to the teams, provide value, and then ask how you can provide more value."*

It's easy to *set* a goal for the community—it's far more difficult to *establish* the goal as something people within the organization truly support. Establishing a goal means everyone needs to know it, believe in it, and change their behavior to support it. The best goals are really specific to the unique needs of individuals within the organization.

The skill-set needed to build an indispensable community is to build relationships with colleagues so they can benefit from these contributions.

BugCrowd

Since graduating in 2008, Sam Houston's career had drifted. In the past decade, he had worked for (or contracted with) 10 different organizations. Even by the mercenary standards of Silicon Valley, 10 community jobs in six years isn't a good look. Houston knew community was important and could be a great asset, but he was never getting the necessary support. He would either leave his employer in frustration when they '*didn't get it*', his contract would expire, or his position would be terminated.

In November 2014, Houston landed a job with Bugcrowd. Bugcrowd began with a $50k seed investment to build '*crowd-sourced security testing for enterprise*'. Enterprise companies set bounties and challenge white-hat (good) hackers to find security flaws in their system. The first hacker to find a flaw gets the bounty. Unlike its competitors, Bugcrowd isn't in *land grab mode* (a term used in Silicon Valley meaning to grab the maximum possible amount of attention at any cost). Bugcrowd is a mature sales-led organization. Net profit is more important than engagement. Responsible spending is the name of the game.

Houston's job was to build and nurture the community of hackers (internally known as researchers) who would find flaws. Although Houston had an advantage (the community is largely the product), he soon found it wasn't easy going:

"I had a tough time at first. The sales team and I didn't get along. I felt they were telling me what to do in the community and what I could tweet about."

Houston was in danger of falling into his same old pattern of frustration. But then something changed his entire approach to work.

"We had a situation where we were trying to acquire one of our competitor's biggest customers. The customer asked our sales person if we had the same hackers in our community as our competitors. Our sales person didn't know so he asked me."

Houston did some quick research and built a list of not only the same hacker profiles in both communities but also how hackers within his community talked about and discussed the competitor. Houston smiles with pride as he recalls:

"Those quotes and profiles became slides that are now used in sales presentations, which have helped us win a lot of new business."

Notice the critical component here. Once Houston understood the *specific* priorities of his colleagues, he could align the community value to match. Even the smallest wins like these help build widespread support for the community. You may think that all sales people only care about leads and conversions, but as Houston's story shows, they also care about their immediate problems, like finding great material for sales presentations. Pulling out quotes, profiles of top researchers, or success stories is a win for Houston, which gains him resources. The sales team, in return, can help promote the community to prospective clients and ask them to check it out before becoming a customer. Houston didn't stop there. Like Shaw and Paredez, he also began to understand the benefit in spending time with people without any agenda, to understand what they are doing.

> *"Sometimes it's as simple as shooting the shit with the engineer after hours. I hear what's going on, I learn their design cycle. I discover things that should be in the design. Now I can figure out useful ways to work with them and use the community to help them get what they need."*

What engineers needed most was a method of getting quick, rapid, feedback, without going through a lengthy, laborious, process. This is a big win for engineers and helped the members feel they were contributing directly to the product. Once Houston knew *exactly* what the sales team and engineering team needed, he could work on helping members make similar contributions. This allowed Houston to set specific goals, such as collecting the names of top hackers and high profile successes for presentations, *indispensable* outcome to his colleagues.

These small victories changed Houston from a frustrated purist to a successful realist. Houston now works to better understand the colleagues he works with and find new ways the community can help them. In return, he finds those departments can help him, too. In the humdrum of community life, there are countless opportunities to show value, build more understanding, and find new ways to help other departments within the company. Each victory helps build momentum and sets the stage for more victories and more buy-in.

Houston's story also illustrates the difference between what the organization wants and what people need. An organization might care about keeping customers active and participating, but his colleagues care about more immediate concerns. Big collective goals are great, but urgent individualistic goals are better. The simple lesson from Houston's experience is to spend time with other teams, really listen to what they need, and adapt the goals to match. This might be a big list of leads, but it can also be case studies, quotes, or images for presentation material. All of this requires an investment in building strong relationships with colleagues. And these relationships don't happen overnight.

Support Is A Slow Dance

When Alex[104] was hired to manage a support community for a major software service provider, she knew she had a challenge on her hands. Most of the service's users weren't aware the company had a support community. It's several clicks deep within the website, hosted on an outdated platform, and was managed by a small team trying to engage with hundreds of thousands of members. Some areas of the community had been left untouched by staff for years and were filled with spam. The company had been steaming forward, but the help community had been left behind.

Alex's challenge was getting her colleagues to understand what a support community is, how it worked, and how it could help them. Her company's internal philosophy centered around showing impact: *"At [company], we don't reward based on how hard you worked, we reward on the impact you've made that benefits your own team and your partners."*

If Alex wanted to get the support from her colleagues, she needed to show the impact the community could have. Yet, in most situations, Alex notes, showing impact often required her colleague's support:

> *"If someone is having trouble reporting a sensitive problem or they're telling us the contact form isn't working the way they want, it would be really difficult for us to escalate these issues to different teams without their support."*

First, Alex needed to get to know her colleagues and build relationships, which is a process. Alex and her team didn't promise the community could definitely help achieve their colleagues' goals, but they looked for common ground where a mutually beneficial alliance could be built to harvest more value from the community. Alex recalls:

> *"I was introduced to [colleague] by my manager. Instead of piling on with my marketing message, we spent an hour talking about his team and processes. I learned what he was*

---

104 Not her real name.

trying to accomplish. He was looking for specific types of feedback. Then the lightbulb went off. Someone on my team is looking at feedback for similar experiences that are broken. We can't get any feedback, not even from employees."

Anna, a member of Alex's team, could easily write a tailored message and get community feedback to solve this problem. Even if this idea wasn't the right fit, it was a common place to explore future possibilities, as Alex elaborates:

"We ended up introducing our team members and got feedback for him. That's not a huge win, it's just one thing they were stuck on."

The foundation of a longer term relationship, the example shows the *impact* of the community. It's one thing to find someone who is willing to help out and give their support for a short time; it's another matter entirely to find common ground to build a lasting mutual alliance that delivers a meaningful impact for both parties. This common ground is identified in the relationship stage and solidified through tiny victories. But the relationships, Alex believes, have to begin the right way:

"If you have no relationship with somebody, they're not going to take the time to walk you through their goals and what they're anxious about. If you go in there thinking, 'I'm going to get my way' or 'we're going to get buy in', you'll lose. It has to be like a true partnership."

Most brand communities may be digital, but relationships are still analogue. Relationships don't have an on/off switch, they're not a binary 1 or a 0. Every relationship exists on a wide spectrum of intensity, depending upon a range of signals and influences. Building a new relationship isn't a one-shot deal. It doesn't happen in a single meeting. It's a slow process, a dance, as Alex calls it.

Once trust is established, it becomes a lot easier to build more successes and ask for more. Each of the alliances Alex builds unlocks more value from the community. Every alliance she builds makes the community increasingly indispensable to her colleagues. In turn, Alex gets the support she needs to execute her vision.

In just two and a half years, Alex has *doubled* the size of her team, expanded coverage into six new languages, and developed processes and systems to deliver influence across the company. Alex's success, she notes, hinges almost entirely upon her and her team's ability to build and evolve relationships, understand what people need, and then deliver on those needs.

Weebly

It's much easier to get support for a brand community when colleagues can see it. It's a lot harder to get support to build a brand community from people who have never seen, nor participated in, a brand community.

In June 2015, Erin Dame pitched the idea of an online community to Weebly's three co-founders during her trial week and got the job as their new community manager. She quickly discovered it was one thing to win over three enthusiastic co-founders who had grown up in the world of online communities; it was another thing entirely to win over skeptical colleagues, some of whom had no idea what a brand community could be.

For a time in the late noughties, Weebly was a classic Silicon Valley success story. Founded by three 22-year-old friends to enable Penn State students to maintain a personal portfolio, it soon morphed into a company that allowed anybody to create and manage a website. It was perfect for small business owners and hobbyists who wanted to pursue their passion without having to hire a web development team. As the saying goes, where attention flows, money follows. Weebly raised further investment rounds in 2011 and 2014,[105] but largely stays under the tech press radar.

Before Dame joined, Weebly had created accounts on Facebook, Twitter, and other platforms. These platforms were great for talking to customers, but terrible for letting customers

---

105 https://www.crunchbase.com/organization/weebly

talk to each other. Dame's mission was to build a community that would let these interactions happen.

Dame soon discovered it's hard to sell the idea of a community to people who have never seen one. She couldn't point to something Weebly already had and say, "*let's do that, but much better.*" If this was going to work, she would have to educate and persuade dozens of skeptical colleagues one by one. This was going to require a lot of support-building.

Dame set aside her first month to do interviews "*with anyone that would talk to me about community.*" In each of these meetings she took detailed notes, learnt about the roles and challenges of colleagues, and began to understand what would help (or at least not hurt) her senior colleagues. She didn't go for the hard sell; she kept an open mind and listened to the genuine concerns of her colleagues.

She discovered every department had different needs from the community. Developers wanted their own developer community, marketers wanted a separation of the community from their existing health center (along with using the community as a brand content distribution channel). Others were concerned about the tone of voice matching the brand voice. While Dame wanted to be friendly, add jokes to emails, and communicate to members in personalized ways, this didn't match the Weebly brand guidelines and would have caused problems.

Customer support had their own goals, too. As Dame explains, they didn't want a *call deflection community* like GiffGaff, "*that implies they want customers to get an answer and leave. They want to engage and invite customers to have discussions with them.*" If the community gives people an answer and then they leave, that's a problem. It's almost the antithesis of the brand's person-ality. Weebly wants to have discussions with customers.

It wasn't easy for Dame to spend an entire month listening to objections, rejections, and a growing list of complications of her community, but it achieved two goals. First, it ensured her senior colleagues had been genuinely listened to and could highlight their concerns and ideas. This increased buy-in for the community. Second, it gave Dame a long list of challenges to overcome and opportunities to seize. She couldn't make the community work for everyone, but now she knew where the community could have the biggest impact and some landmines to avoid.

This is the hard, invaluable, work that makes an indispensable community. Dame worked to build her internal allies and ensure the community could be tremendously useful. She also tackled people who had no idea what a community was or what it could do:

> *"I started with asking what communities they were a part of. How they replied would help me understand what they know of community at the moment. There is a big difference from saying Reddit than saying Facebook. Then I took people down a path, to persuade them they knew more about community than they thought they did."*

This was more successful with some than others, but most seemed more open to the idea afterwards. Once they understood the concept of community (people talking to and helping one another online), they could begin to connect it to ways that would help them. By the end of the year, Dame had gained at least one solid ally in each major department (marketing, analytics, engineering, design, etc...).

> *"It took a lot of internal support to make that happen, about a full year. When I came in, not many people knew what a community was. It took six months to get the support and another six months on a fast-track build [creating the website]."*

Today, her community is well-funded and racks up regular customer wins. Internal staff brag about the community, talk about it at Weebly's events, and most staff members know its value to customers. This community also helps Weebly do useful things, like guiding members through the process of setting up a website at community events. Most importantly, the community has saved Weebly *half a million dollars* in support costs in its first year alone.

It would have been far easier for Dame to start the community on day one without working internally with her colleagues. Dame could have used a free platform, started inviting customers she knew to use it, and tried to get activity up. This would have led *directly* into the engagement trap. She would have been the *engagement person* who spends her time feeling frustrated that her colleagues *don't get it.*

Instead, Dame built internal alliances, uncovering the priorities of her colleagues, and aligning the community to match. Once she had the support of colleagues throughout the organization, she could start to expand the scope of the community. She's slowly making herself indispensable.

Autodesk, Element14, and Hubris

Lois Townsend, Autodesk's former Director of Social Media and Community, can scarcely imagine losing the community. *"It would be dark, very dark," she says.*

Autodesk, a maker of software for architecture, engineering, and construction industries, has a behemoth of a brand community. It's more accurate to describe it as a vast ecosystem, a digital city perhaps, hosting hundreds of distinct communities—communities for 3D animators, educators, industrial designers, simulators, and makers, where Autodesk's customers collaborate, share advice, and learn to create better videos, designs, and products.

The ecosystem hosts an incredible 70+ support communities covering every one of Autodesk's products and services. Members help answer one another's questions without ever having to call customer support. It also hosts Autodesk Expert Elite, where top experts are motivated and rewarded for answerings thousands of customer questions every month; the Autodesk Developer Network, for developers to swap tips; and Autodesk Labs, where customers can test new features and share what they like. It even includes IdeaStation, for customers to share product ideas and vote on which they like best. The ecosystem also transverses language barriers with separate communities in Chinese,

French, German, Japanese, Portuguese, Russian, Spanish, and Turkish.

If the community were to vanish tomorrow, Autodesk would also lose their most powerful tools for learning what their customers want and need. They wouldn't get immediate warnings on product bugs to fix, nor stay close to the pulse of what their members really need. They may even have to go back to, as Townsend describes, *"slow, costly, focus groups."*

Equally worrying, tens of millions of dollars in annual search traffic would disappear. Thousands of prospective customers would never buy the software. Even the advocacy program, Autodesk Expert Elite, which has nurtured 400+ brand ambassadors from 53 countries, would vanish.

Autodesk would lose thousands of customers answering tens of thousands of questions every month. All the past solutions, which help millions of customers every day, would disappear, too. Townsend summarised the outcome simply. Without the community, Autodesk would have *"no way to serve millions of customers."* The AutoDesk community team might be forgiven for thinking their work was indispensable.

Townsend was right, although it is hard to imagine losing the community, Autodesk was willing to lose many of the staff working on the community.

In 2017, after the arrival of a new CEO, the community team was downsized and the budget cut. Several staff members who felt secure in their jobs suddenly found themselves out of work. The community was still delivering the same results, but the perceived value of those results had changed. Once again, when a brand looked to reduce costs, the community team was among the first to be cut. The Autodesk community still provided the same value as before, but the perception of this value had shifted. The perceived value of the community didn't compare well with the value from other brands.

Ensuring a company perceives the community as high value is not a one-time effort. It's constant and ongoing. It won't show up in the job description, but it's a critical part of the job. New bosses will always be arriving with different experiences and new priorities. If they don't soon see the value of the community, and that value isn't supported throughout the organization, the community becomes an immediate target to save money.

Dianne Kibbey knows this better than most. In 2009, she was recruited from Premier Farnell's eCommerce team to start *Element14*,[106] an online community for electronic engineers. Premier Farnell is a global distributor of electronic components selling two million products from 3,000 different manufacturers. Their main customers are electronic design engineers. These engineers used Premier Farnell products to design and sell their own products.[107]

Unlike most companies, the impetus for the community came from the company's CEO. Kibbey, relying upon her eCommerce background, set the early goals of the community based upon what she knew and understood: click-throughs and sales. These metrics, Kibbey notes, were essential to getting sign-off from the board, but came with a downside.

> *"This succeeded in driving mass registrations and a lot of traffic, but also lots of people who didn't come back and some who didn't know why they were there [...] We became very focused on vanity metrics such as registrations and click-throughs vs. those that signify a healthy vibrant community."*

When Kibbey's CEO left in 2012, she found herself having to prove the value of the community again. A big round of layoffs soon followed and the community team took one of the biggest hits. Kibbey needed to again understand what senior leadership wanted and deliver those results. This time around, the focus became participation metrics (i.e. real discussions, members asking questions, and solving each other's problems).

Another change of CEO in 2016 required a revamp of the community goals to focus on suppliers and getting products into the hand of members. Another CEO in 2018 might well

---

106 The 14th element in the periodic table is silicon, the key component in most designs.

107 https://vimeo.com/147555509

change the goals again. Over time, Kibbey has come to realize the key is continuing to keep and gain support.

"You really do need to know what the hot button is with your senior management teams. When click-throughs and sales were a huge obsession, I reported on these topics and focused on new customer acquisition. Now the focus on involving our suppliers in our community is really important [...] I try to focus on how many suppliers we're working with. Are we developing programs that really make sense of the community and for them?"

Kibbey keeps the community close to the pulse of what her senior leaders care about. In turn, she's found they now believe the community is one of the company's great unique selling points. She increasingly gets pulled into meetings with suppliers as the community provides them with a unique place to showcase products. It took a lot of understanding on her part and education of senior supporters, but she's gradually made herself indispensable.

"In the distribution business your strategic suppliers work with you to determine the products you stock, pricing, etc. They are all coming to us to find ways to participate in Element 14."

Summary

Becoming indispensable isn't an option, it's a necessity for builders of brand communities. Communities don't have the same obvious impact as sales, marketing, and PR, so everyone building a brand community needs to work to establish the biggest impact they can have and ensure they deliver that impact.

Impact typically begins with small victories. But these small victories require strong relationships. It takes time to build a relationship. It has to begin with honest intentions and a genuine curiosity to understand what colleagues are struggling with, what they want to achieve, and identify where the community can help. The impact is usually very specific. A series of small victories over a long time can build a powerful alliance.

As the community expands, the community often moves beyond tiny impacts and towards bigger goals, like a broader organizational change or pursuing the organization's mission. As Kibbey discovered, long term, the secret is to stay very close to the pulse of what senior leaders care about—to find out what they care about and design the community around those goals. This can take time. Kibbey is going on a decade and it's not a one-shot effort. Kibbey has constantly been knocked back by major staff changes. Autodesk's community showed that no community is too big to have their resources cut. It's an ongoing, never ending, process.

CHAPTER 10

GO FURTHER TOGETHER

In 2012, FeverBee tried to find out the success rate of brand communities. How many of those launched to great fanfare over the past eight years still existed? After browsing through 700+ press releases excitedly announcing the launch of a community, just five of the communities still had any meaningful level of activity, a success rate of 0.7%.[108] Clearly, the paid professionals were struggling.

Five years later, FeverBee teamed up with Jacqueline Pike, associate professor at the Palumbo Donahue School of Business, to study 190 online communities created and run by amateurs (those managing a community as an unpaid hobby). This was one of the largest comparable community data sets ever studied and covered tens of millions of posts from hundreds of thousands of members (63% had more than 100 participants). Survivorship bias is certainly a factor here. It's hard to analyze communities that have died and vanished. But it's also reasonably clear communities founded by amateurs are more likely to succeed than those built by paid professionals.

Consider for a second just how remarkable this is. People building communities in their spare time, with limited resources, are more likely to succeed than companies with a full-time community manager and all the resources of an organization. *How can this be happening?*

Amateurs may not have the resources, but they have the freedom to develop the community in any way that suits themselves or their audience. Hobbyists build communities to enjoy themselves.

---

108 We should caveat this by saying many brands don't issue press releases when they launch a community.

They don't need to have a big launch. They don't have to show impact. They can grow the community slowly. They can say whatever they want and let members do (almost) whatever they want, too. Speed and freedom are powerful allies for an amateur.

Communities created by professionals get tangled up in a web of their own restraints. They often make the community about themselves. They spend huge fortunes on a platform and wait months for it to be ready. They may force members to do things they don't want to do. If they don't hit specific targets by specific dates, the community typically gets canned.

It isn't that amateurs are *better* than professionals at building communities, but amateurs have the advantage of being able to do whatever they want, while paid professionals are restricted by what the organization lets them do. The paid pros endure all of the constraints of working for their organization while rarely getting to enjoy the benefits. And these benefits could be *huge.*

If the professionals could bring to bear their full armament of resources, it wouldn't even be a close fight; they would thrash the amateurs every time. For example, a fan may be able to create a community about Adobe's Photoshop and invite people they know to join it. But a community manager working at Adobe can, theoretically, invite *every Adobe customer on the planet to join in a single email.* A fan might allow people to say what they don't like about Photoshop, but a community manager at Adobe can put these people directly in touch with the company's engineers to fix their problems. Members could see their recommendations being implemented.

Every organization has far more resources they could (and should) commit to their community. Many ways every department can support a community are too frequently ignored. Imagine each department as an engine cylinder and the community as the rocket ship. Getting these cylinders fired up, bringing to bear the organization's full resources, is critical to success when building an *indispensable community.* Support doesn't just mean money, it means permission, access, expertise, technical support, and connections. Most people never ask for the most valuable things.

For example, one FeverBee client achieved a 50% boost in membership simply by asking to have the community featured more prominently on the company website, something they had never thought to do before. Another had a big win by asking the PR team to reach out to industry celebs to participate in community activities.

This chapter is about using every single asset a brand has available to ensure the community succeeds. It's about not just getting kind words of support but getting resources to help build the community. A colleague *showing* support is very different from a colleague *giving* support. Support isn't kind, positive, words towards a community. Most people like the idea of having a brand community and senior leaders are expected to motivate their team by saying positive, encouraging, words. Real support boils down to resources. Until a colleague sacrifices a resource (time, staff, money, etc...) to help the community, that support doesn't exist.

Joel, a community manager of a non-profit in Idaho, learned this the hard way. Joel spent months building a case for a new platform. He identified user stories, compared vendors, justified the expense, and finally got the budget he needed. Just when it was about to be a done deal, Joel was told *"the department is too low risk"* and funds were diverted to higher risk areas. He hadn't properly understood the priorities of the finance team. He had confused a show of support with getting the resources.

At a community conference in 2016, one speaker declared her members were several times more likely to complete their free trial (and pay for a month's membership). This, she exclaimed, proved the value of the community and got senior leadership on their side. Sadly, a year later, when the budget became tight, the entire community team was released.

A community goal is never truly established until colleagues are sacrificing their time, money, expertise, and resources to support it. It's a lot easier to get 2,000 customers to join and participate in a community than to find 20 colleagues who will help build one. As we saw in the previous chapter, the community has to provide something other departments want. This means building strong internal alliances.

Imagine we want the PR team to promote the community. The chances are they're too busy with too many other priorities. It would be a miracle to get a mention in a press release, let alone mainstream media coverage. It might be possible to string together the right combination of words to get resources, but it's unlikely. They might help promote the community if the community provides them with great product success stories from members, identifies interesting new trends, highlights remarkable personalities they can put in front of the media, or identifies possible PR crises before they blow up. If we go back to our rocket ship metaphor, this is the *fuel* they need to support the community. If the community helps the PR team, it makes sense for the PR team to promote the community. And PR teams can drive a lot of traffic and new members to the community. When a PR team is fired up and promoting the community to thousands, if not millions, of people, everybody wins.

The best way to *get support* is always to *give support*. This works with every department. The sales team might drive new customers to the community if the community provides them 30 good sales leads. Any brand community can invite members to ask pre-purchase questions and get honest responses from members. In return, the sales team can drive more people to the community. After they buy, customers can be directed to the community for help learning to use the product. It's a mutual win.

Likewise, the HR team can embed community participation as a core principle for staff members if the community can help them train employees, understand what members want, and reduce the time to get a new employee up to speed. They might even be willing to use the community as a recruiting platform. Members can share job adverts within their network, for example.

The more departments that support the community, the more successful the community will be. Supporting a brand community with more resources should be a no-brainer. Getting support is rarely the rest of what's said in the meeting; it's about what the community manager *brings* into the meeting. Is it 20 sales leads? Fifty case studies? Five interested job applicants?

Support always comes down to the level of resources others are willing to part with to make the brand community thrive. Kind words aren't worth much when the budget axe swings. Every department can commit more to the community than they do. And the only way a community thrives is with more resources. If the community is the rocketship, each department is an engine cylinder you need to fuel to blast into the stratosphere.

Xbox

Ivory Harvey had recently transitioned from a customer support role (*"answering as many questions as you can"*) to the Xbox community ambassador program. Now she was part of a dozen-strong team, which included a mix of community managers, coordinators, and developers. And she soon found herself under pressure to deliver more from Xbox fans.

The ambassador program was launched in 2011 to get fans to answer community questions, both in the Xbox forum and elsewhere (mostly Reddit). The program was designed to motivate and reward top community members for helping other gamers. Xbox could simply give away free swag, but Harvey knew free swag wasn't a big motivator.

The biggest motivator would be feeling actively engaged with Xbox itself. Harvey explains this isn't something you can fake:

> *"You can't trick people [ambassadors], they have to actually meet and connect with senior people within the organization to feel their voices are being heard."*

But this meant people from various departments outside of the immediate community team would have to sacrifice their time to work with ambassadors. She had to persuade busy colleagues she had no authority over to help her out.

It didn't begin well. Most people replied with, *"oh, that's cute, but it's not really for us."* But Harvey persisted until she found someone who would listen:

> *"After being told 'no' a bunch of times, I decided we would find champions in each space who inherently believed in the*

community. They weren't the most senior people, but they were the people who believed in the community and were passionate about what we were doing."

Part of the secret, she discovered, was time. Confronting people with a new idea and expecting them to leap aboard wasn't realistic. Relationships take time to build and new ideas need time to settle. But Harvey wasn't sure how much time she had.

Then she met a general manager at the Xbox live marketing and product team who adopted the ambassador program as his pet project. Together, they set up a system whereby ambassadors could now ask their questions directly to marketing managers and play games with the people who made the games. For ambassadors, nothing was more motivating than feeling important, listened to, and having exclusive access.

Harvey notes it's not uncommon for ambassadors to challenge the Xbox Live marketing managers to a 30-minute Xbox Halo match. Ambassadors have also started to follow the team on social channels, which helps spread the right messages, gather feedback, and improve the product.

In March 2017, the Xbox team was about to release a huge update, changing the navigation and layout of the platform for comparison, imagine someone walking into your house and rearranging the furniture). Updates like these often cause a backlash while people struggle to adjust to the new layout. To tackle this, Harvey and her team provided ambassadors with information, links, and support articles on the community, created by both themselves and community members, and asked them to share them across social channels. Ambassadors were asked to identify potential issues.

Unlike previous updates, the talk from the community was largely positive. People shared useful messages that aligned with the very messages the marketing team wants to see. This small victory created a great story across marketing and other departments that the community existed.

Later, with the Xbox Game pass (a subscription service that lets gamers play a variety of different games), the marketing live team put the game quickly into the hands of ambassadors and asked them to share their experiences. As Harvey proclaims:

"Over time, we've seen great video content, great streaming content, great articles, and great engagement. They [the ambassadors] really helped evangelize the product."

As Harvey has shown with the Xbox ambassador platform, the secret to getting more value from the community isn't more people. There's a finite number of people that will ever join any community. The secret to unlocking the most value was to take the time (in this case, a lot of time) to build those internal alliances and find something to offer those departments. As a result, she helped build a community only Xbox could create, a community with no competition where ambassadors can engage directly with the people making and marketing the game.

Faster Alone, Further Together

The danger with focusing on the people who support the community is ignoring those who don't, especially the *silent detractors.* Many people are hard to predict but can react ferociously when they feel the community is treading on their turf. They are the *detractors.*

The obvious detractors are easy to spot—the legal, HR, and financial teams who have the power to kill the community if it seems a threat. Others include engineers, PR, marketing, and customer support who might step in if the community gets in their path. It's easy to ignore the detractors. Maybe if they keep to their lane, and we keep to ours, everything will be ok. In an expansive community, that's difficult.

The list of people who can be affected by a community is longer than we might imagine. It includes anyone who might feel the community intrudes on their turf, competes with the community for resources, or dislikes the level of attention the community is receiving. The following is a list of situations FeverBee has encountered in the past decade:

- A marketing team worried when members share information the company hasn't announced yet;

- The same marketing team upset the community manager wasn't sticking to the community brand;
- Customer support worried the community was causing the number of tickets to *drop* (they feared their budget might be cut);
- Web/IT staff worried about having another big tech integration project dropped on them without being allowed to hire more staff to deal with it;
- A procurement team that bought the cheapest possible web platform without any consideration for the user experience and refused to change it;
- A legal department that briefly shut the community down in Europe because of new data privacy laws and refused to explain to members why;
- A legal team that refused to allow competitions and stopped rewarding ambassadors lest they be considered employees;
- A video production group that threatened to quit when members began sharing their home-made product videos in the community;
- An HR department that refused to let employees participate in the community and only relented if all communications were approved by them first;
- A CFO who would only accept sales driven from the community as a viable metric.

These scenarios are why trying to fly under the radar doesn't end well. People don't like to be surprised. The natural response to a surprise is to look for the danger. It's easy to find danger in a community. It's easy to dismiss the concerns above, perhaps consider these departments as outdated and say they just don't get community. But such concerns are legitimate.

It might seem crazy for an HR team not to allow staff to participate, but it's far worse when *Business Insider* quotes a jokey post by a community staffer as an official brand position. This can blow up into a PR disaster with huge repercussions. It might not seem logical for the legal team to refuse ambassadors rewards, but AOL was successfully sued for $15m by volunteers claiming they were technically employed.[109] If the objections above seem minor and mean-spirited, it's often because colleagues are looking at the bigger picture.

The head of the customer support team didn't want support tickets to drop because he hated the idea of laying off staff with Christmas approaching. Every concern is completely legitimate in its own way and can be addressed if enough time is taken to engage with each department. It's a bad idea to surprise people or assume who will or won't be interested in the community.

The best community builders don't try to skirt around the people and problems they don't like—they tackle them directly. They proactively reach out, build bridges, and try to address possible concerns. A professional *deals with problems before they arise.*

It's tempting to ignore the objectors, but it's always a mistake. Any one of them can become the next CEO or at least a big influencer over what happens. It's telling that both Maria Ogneva from LinkedIn and Sam Houston at Bugcrowd used the exact same quote:

"You can go faster alone, but you will go further together."

WellsFargo

Kathleen McMahon arrived on her first day of work at WellsFargo to find a struggling community with limited activity and a demoralized team. McMahon promised she could attract 30,000 monthly visitors to the dormant community. Although she *"didn't know how [she] would do it,"* she trusted herself to figure it out. But now she wasn't so sure.

When she ran into the bank's risk officer, he told her *"We're uncomfortable with this whole thing and I'm going to clamp down hard on you."* McMahon smiles wryly as she recalls, *"He was a straight-laced ex-military guy. He would tell me things like, you can't put the word 'or' in that context."*

---

109 https://archives.cjr.org/the_news_frontier/aol_settled_with_unpaid_volunt.php

To understand why building a community at organizations like WellsFargo is so challenging, it's helpful to understand Unfair, Deceptive, or Abusive Acts Practices (UDAAP) compliance. UDAAP is a huge swathe of legislation, which came into force as part of the Dodd-Frank Act after the 2008 financial crisis. Consumers must have access to reliable and trustworthy information that lets them make the best decisions for their situation. Banks like WellsFargo must avoid publishing or facilitating the exchange of incorrect information.

The keyword here is *facilitating*. What happens if a bank hosts a community in which members share false information?

Like many aspects of law, it's open to degrees of interpretation, but banks would rather not take the risk at all. Most have hired a large team of compliance professionals, under the banner of governance, to minimize the risk of violating this law. And McMahon was about to run straight into governance.

The irony for McMahon is, the more successful the community becomes, the riskier it is and the bigger the odds of being shut down. The more content members share, the more likely it is that it will be incorrect and increase the risk to WellsFargo. If technology startups are fertile breeding grounds for community, growing a community at a bank is like growing crops on the surface of the moon.

McMahon had a choice. She could either accept the community as it was and muddle along *or* she could fight like hell to make the community something that, a) didn't feel risky, b) customers wanted to participate in, and c) would be valuable to WellsFargo.

McMahon had one natural weapon at her disposal, *her personality*. Unlike many community pros, McMahon was older, more experienced, and a natural people person. She comes across as a friendly, formidable, pragmatist who is more comfortable meeting people in person than having an endless back and forth via email. In some community roles, this might be a hindrance, but at WellsFargo it was an indispensable asset.

McMahon began by taking the objecting risk officer to lunch, followed by many more lunches. She was determined to learn from him and show him she understood and appreciated the risks. She didn't just listen, she adapted her approach to accommodate his concerns. As she explains: "*I couldn't go in there [a meeting] without knowing what their concerns were. I had to understand not only their concerns but also how we were going to make sure not to trip those concerns. [...] It was more far more important to understand than be understood.*"

McMahon arrived at every meeting prepared not just with her plans but also with clear steps to minimize the risk and counter any objections they might have. Integrating a response to the concerns into the project itself went a long way to getting the permission to grow the community. The second step was to change the topic. The current community focus, *student lending*, was a non-starter. McMahon wanted to cover customer support instead. Her first pitch was brutally shot down, but she had a plan...*an exit plan.*

> "*They told me they already have a phone for that. So I decided to take baby steps. I asked them to let me try it a month, if it doesn't work we'll stop. I even created an exit plan in case it didn't work out.*"

Creating an exit plan for a community that didn't even exist yet might sound like overkill but it demonstrated exactly the obsessive attention to detail McMahon's risk-aware colleague needed to feel safe. McMahon's entire aim was to reduce the level of risk to as close to zero as possible.

This kind of obsessive listening and understanding of her colleague's concerns takes time. McMahon estimates she spends a remarkable 80% of her hours working inside her organization compared with working with members of the community. Yet this is the only way a community at such an organization can succeed. It takes a colossal amount of trust.

Today, the community continues to grow in size and activity. It might be hosted on a separate website and prevent customers from answering each other's questions (all questions receive a staff response), but it exists and is active. It's a place where customers can go to ask questions and WellsFargo can answer them. The community's very existence is a tribute to the incredible power of investing time to understand colleagues and then adapt a plan based upon those concerns. By building and constantly tending to these relationships, McMahon was able to gain the support she needed to build a community.

Summary

A community has the potential to be an incredible strategic asset that supports every area of the business. But that will only happen if it gets the support of people throughout the organization. Support isn't what people say, it's what resources they commit.

The more resources a community receives, the more successful it will become. A brand community can give members direct access to staff and colleagues, drive more traffic, attract top experts, build a terrific platform, and much more. But this requires people throughout the business supporting the community.

Alliances can't be built on just words—the community has to come up with the goods. The best alliances are those where it's in both parties' interests to commit resources because they get more back from it. This is what happens when a PR team promotes a community that provides them with more case studies. It's a flywheel that spins faster and faster.

A community is so broad and expansive that it naturally treads on the turf of others—not just in the battle for resources, but in the actions of members, the legal liabilities, PR implications, customer support outcomes and much more. Surprising these departments with a new community doesn't pan out well. Instead, they need to be brought along in the process. They need to be proactively engaged, understood, and incorporated into the plan.

Making a community indispensable to our colleagues involves being realistic and understanding that the community has to deliver results, understanding the results it can deliver, and then building relationships to make those results possible. Every relationship increases the potential value of the community for everyone and brings the community one step closer to becoming *indispensable.*

Chapter 11

DESIGNING AN INDISPENSABLE COMMUNITY

According to Colleen Young, Mayo Clinic Connect was suffering from the "Mayfly Effect".

The swarms of Mayflies (small flying insects) that descend upon Eastern Canada and the United States each year blanket every car, sidewalk, and surface in their path. But their remarkable conquest is short-lived. After 24 hours of unstoppable revelry, they die, leaving residents to clean up millions, possibly billions, of carcasses. Young found her new community in a similar state.

Mayo Clinic, a nonprofit academic medical center, launched *Mayo Connect* in July 2011, as part of a larger social media presence. The community was an immediate success. Within the first quarter, it had surpassed its membership projections for the entire year. But, Young notes, they "hadn't planned for this success." There was no follow-up act or long-term plan to build powerful relationships between members. Soon the novelty wore off. Activity began to slow down, priorities shifted, and the community was left with the digital carcasses of tens of thousands of members. It was well on its way to the internet scrapheap when Young arrived in 2015.

Young faced a nearly impossible challenge. There aren't many successful second acts in the history of brand communities and the web is littered with the expensive remnants of those who have tried. The odds were stacked against her. Mayo Connect was hosted on archaic technology. No one had made a serious attempt to engage members for years. It wasn't even clear how many members still visited the community. Young needed to rebuild support from her colleagues, some of whom now used the community solely as a place to send news updates to the disengaged masses.

A Community Strategy Drives Big Wins

Young wasn't a newcomer to community. She had hard-won expertise from the Canadian Cancer Society and Canadian Virtual Hospice. She had about as much experience in building health-related communities as anyone. Using these skills to bring the community back to life, she created discussions, ensured every post received a response, and helped members connect with one another. Activity began to increase but it was unrelentingly difficult work.

Working harder isn't a sustainable strategy. There are only so many hours in a day, only so many discussions that can be created and responded to, and only so many members who can be greeted. Engaging members with enthusiasm can bring the metrics up, but it's not driving it to its full potential. A strategy isn't a plan to do things better. That's just a list of tactics (combined with a dash of wishful thinking). A strategy determines what really moves the needle and then uses all available resources (budget, time, and knowledge, etc...) to make it happen. To use a military metaphor, a military strategist doesn't try to *do better* in every battle. A military strategist decides that battles are worth fighting and allocates every possible resource to win those battles decisively.

For example, it's one thing to invite top members to become community leaders and run their own groups in the community. It's another to set aside a budget to support them (Wikimedia) or fly them from around the world to meet with your team and advise you (Spotify/EVE Online). Members are a lot more likely to step forward and become leaders when they feel supported and respected by the brand. But this costs more money that has to come from somewhere else. In a strategy platform determines what has to give way.

Deep down, most people consider themselves an expert strategist. They think they can create a better strategy for their community, even their business, than whatever already exists. Yet few people ever manage to do it. They might create the strategy, but then *something happens* and it's never executed. You might be able to hammer out a 50-page strategy, but real strategists get their strategies implemented. Far too many community strategies begin collecting digital dust from the day they're created.

Young had seen this first hand. She had created a few digital-dust collectors in her time. She had followed a template, tried to make everything fit, but, she explains, it didn't quite work out.

> *"It was just a huge exercise to create a document, trying to fill in the blanks of a template that didn't really fit, knowing the whole time that no one would take the time to read it [...]. I didn't get more backing for the community based on the strategy. It was just another situation of 'oh god, what are you actually trying to do?'"*

Most strategies are too long for anyone to read. At the end of FeverBee's first community management course, in 2011, attendees were asked to send in their strategy. The average strategy was over fifty pages long (about half the length of a typical non-fiction book). It was a nightmare. Longer and more detailed strategies are typically less flexible. When 'something changes', as it inevitably does in all organizations, the entire strategy becomes redundant.

Five years later, FeverBee launched a new course, Strategic Community Management (attended by Young). The new course made a crucial change—the entire strategic plan could now fit onto a single page. The feedback was markedly better. Participants reported getting better internal support and actually implementing their strategies.

Setting Goals

Realists know a community has to deliver on goals colleagues care abouts. BugCrowd, Swiftkey, LinkedIn, Facebook, and FitBit all show effective community goals come from colleagues. They come from people who usually care far less about a distant measure of *return on investment (ROI)* and far more about anything that helps them save time, save money, or achieve better results *today*. This is where the strategy process begins.

Sometimes goals are dropped on the community by whomever is paying the tab or 'the boss'. Mayo Clinic Connect lived within a bigger social media team, but it was initiated by marketing.[110] While marketing may benefit from more community members booking appointments, Young knew that wasn't the Mayo Clinic's mission.

There are 5,534 registered hospitals in the USA and Mayo Clinic has ranked number 1 amongst them for the past two years[111] (and in the top 3 for the past 28 years[112]). It's been listed among the top 100 places to work for the past 25 years (no easy feat for a hospital). Mayo Clinic owes this success to its unique approach to patient care: the patient is an *equal* part of the healthcare team. They bring as much expertise about their condition as the frontline staff. They know how they *feel* about treatment plans and health goals, and which they're most likely to comply with. They serve as partners in the process.

The great advantage of working for a nonprofit is profit is naturally less important, but having an impact is still critical to employees. Before setting goals, Colleen needed to speak to her colleagues and understand their challenges.

Plenty of strategic advice begins with *list the goal of your community*. But what happens if the community doesn't have goals? What happens if colleagues disagree on the goal? What happens if the stated goal clearly isn't suited to the community? Goals evolve over time too.

One approach to uncovering goals is to be systematic. For instance, one could build a list of all stakeholders and interview each of them. By the end, you'll usually capture the hopes, fears,

---

110 The community now lives with the Social Digital Innovation team in the Public Affairs department. The marketing department remains an ally.

111 www.usnews.com/info/blogs/press-room/articles/2017-08-08/ us-news-announces-2017-18-best-hospitals#close-modal

112 https://health.usnews.com/best-hospitals/area/mn/ mayo-clinic-6610451

dreams, and thoughts of each person who can help or harm the community. Then, selecting goals becomes a simple matter of picking from the list (typically the person with the most interest and influence over the community).

Direct manager	• *Wants to be able to "send a list of great leads to the sales team" and "calculate the value of those leads"* • *Wants to be seen as someone who "gets things done"* • *Worried about people getting in her way*
Director (above line manager)	• *Worried about PR disasters and negative customer feedback reaching the press/the exec team* • *Wants to see better media coverage*
Director of Marketing	• *Wants to increase sales* • *Worried about declining reach of mailing lists*
CEO	• *Wants the company to look innovative* • *Likes to present new technology at events*
Legal Rep.	• *Doesn't want anyone to 'go rogue'* • *Wants people to appreciate the legal risks and not be seen as 'nagging people'*
CFO	• *Wants to find ways to save money.*

In the client example above, the interviews revealed the community manager's boss wanted great sales leads, to know the value of those sales leads, and be seen as someone who gets things done. The community manager's boss' boss wanted to avoid PR disasters and negative customer feedback. The director of marketing wanted to increase sales and was worried about declining reach, and so on. Any one of these can serve as a great goal. As the community expands, it can tackle more goals with more resources.

Young discovered she had allies who felt patients would be much better at coping and recovering from their condition if they could build relationships with others going through the same challenges as them. She also discovered a split. Some colleagues were genuinely interested in building relationships between members, while others were more interested in sending information to members. The goals of the latter wouldn't be a good fit.

Young's discussions revealed clearly the goal needed to be improving the health and wellbeing of members—not just patients, but anyone going through what she calls "*a health journey*" today. Once goals were set, Young began receiving interest from healthcare practitioners eager to recommend the community to their patients, too. They could see the value in it because *they had told Young the value of it*. The next step would be to turn these goals into specific objectives.

ALLIES Don't Want To Be Assets

Young could have tried to drive a lot of engagement, hoping that would help members improve their health, but that's casino thinking. It might happen by chance, but it's unlikely (and leaving anything to chance is a terrible strategy). Young needed to be clear and specific about the behavior she wanted. She needed objectives.

If goals are what colleagues get from the community, objectives are what members need to do to achieve these goals. They are the beloved key performance indicators (*KPIs*) of a community. If members are performing these behaviors often, the community is on the right track. If they're not, it's a problem—regardless of how much activity takes place within the community.

Community members are frustratingly ambivalent about showing up on the balance sheet (or showing any impact at all). They're too preoccupied with the immediate challenges they face today. They want to solve their problems and achieve their goals. They want to feel more socially connected, important, and in control of their future. If a brand community can help them do that better than anywhere else, they will participate. If it can't, they won't... *balance sheet be damned!*

The inevitable conflict at the heart of building any type of brand community is a battle to carefully balance what members

Goal	Objectives Behavior that achieves that goal
Increase customer retention/loyalty	• Asking product questions and getting quick feedback • Reading information about the product's superiority • Reading advice on getting more from the product • Using the product/service with friends • Earning points or status that make switching difficult
Generate new business/find new customers	• Creating content that attracts high search traffic • Sharing problems that self-identify the member as a good lead • Downloading product information that self-identifies the member as a useful lead • Asking pre-purchase related questions • Searching for product information
Advocacy/ spreading word of mouth	• Sharing community content with friends • Writing reviews and testimonials
Reducing customer support	• Asking product questions in the community • Answering product questions in the community • Searching for the answer in the community • Tagging, updating, and documenting product questions
Generating Product Ideas	• Suggesting new idea • Posting product feedback • Voting on ideas • Participating in focus groups • Responding to surveys
Increasing Reach/Reducing Advertising Costs	• Subscribing to the mailing list • Opening emails from the brand • Clicking on links in the email
Recruitment	• Answering questions that demonstrate expertise • Viewing job advertisements posted in the community • Sharing job advertisements posted in the community

Goal	Objectives Behavior that achieves that goal
Improving productivity / reducing dupli-cation of costs	• Asking for help in the community instead of via email • Answering questions in the community • Tagging and sharing documents • Tagging people with skills and expertise • Updating documents • Inviting people to share their expertise
Donations / fundraising / collective actions	• Starting a petition • Signing a petition • Sending a donation • Raising money from friends
Better informed members (non-profit)	• Asking questions in the community about personal challenges • Posting personal experiences • Reading the experiences of others

with what the company needs. If a community skews too heavily toward what members want, it becomes a casino. It might get a lot of activity, but the value of the activity is questionable (FunVille). If the community skews too heavily towards what the brand needs, it becomes a ghost town. It's not interesting enough for members to stay.

Young needed to thread the needle between what her members wanted and colleagues needed. Many organizations have been in Mayo Clinic's position. They've rushed to launch their community without setting objectives, without deciding what members need to do. When the community doesn't show the impact it needs, the community managers double down on engagement. That's a one-way trip into *the engagement trap*.

Every goal needs to be directly translated into very specific member behaviors. As the table above shows, there are plenty of behaviors to choose from for almost any goal.

This is far from a comprehensive list, but you get the idea. Every tactic, every effort to engage members, should drive these behaviors. This is the point of creating a strategy plan. It's not enough for a community if employees have a goal of improving productivity. It needs employees asking questions instead of emailing each other, answering questions in the community, or updating documents in the community. These are the specific behaviors to encourage.

Young knew her members wouldn't suddenly begin managing their diseases better or following treatment plans unless they were asked to do something specific. After speaking with her members, she came up with two specific objectives:

1) Set their own goals for improving how they manage, cope, or recover from their condition; return to the community to report progress.
2) Use their experience and expertise to answer questions from members; share their personal stories where possible.

But did her members want to adopt these behaviors? More specifically, did members have the time, skill, and motivation to perform the behaviors? It's common to treat the community as a vast, homogenous, group with identical needs and motivations. It's also a big mistake. Every member is an individual with different levels of time, talent, and motivation to contribute. Threading the needle begins with what the organization needs, and then we thread what members have the time, talent, and motivation to do. Young set two unique objectives for her two main groups of members: her superusers and her newcomers.

Goal(s)	IMPROVE THE HEALTH AND WELLBEING OF MEMBERS	
Objectives	Get *new members* to set goals and share progress.	Get *top members* (those who have been through treatment) to answer questions and share their experiences

Now she had objectives that aligned with her goal and matched what her members could do.

Objectives for members have to be specific to the unique groups (or segments) that already exist within the community. It's possible to divide a community into dozens of unique groups by activity or interest. But each group requires a lot of resources. Each objective has its own strategy and set of tactics. That's a lot of work.

A solo community manager, like Young, might want to create more groups but she might not have the resources to support them. Two to three unique segments is the most a solo brand community manager can handle. For the Mayo Clinic, two or three would also probably be enough. Young finally had her objectives. She knew what she needed her members to do and what they could do. The next challenge was getting them to do it.

Strategies

Young needed several strategies, one for each objective. She didn't want to build yet another community where people come, ask a question, and leave when they get an answer. She wanted a strategy to keep people hooked, a strategy that would provide the kind of value only Mayo Connect could offer, a strategy to make members feel the emotions that would achieve the objectives.

Community strategies, like all strategies, sit in the middle between objectives and tactics. They take the behaviors members need to perform and provide the motivation to perform them. That *motivation* is always about emotions. Strategies are ultimately about which emotions to amplify to move people to action. Facts can convince people to hold the right kind of beliefs about the community, but emotions persuade people to participate.

It's also at the emotional level where members get the indispensable benefit from being a part of a community. A good brand community can alleviate frustration, help members feel connected and part of something special, and give people joy from helping others. Young needed to identify those emotions.

The key behavior for her newcomers was to set their own goals and report their progress over time. But what kind of emotion drives members to do this? When in doubt, it's easiest to find the most similar examples. Mayo Connect isn't the first community to ask members to set goals and report progress, many fitness communities do too. The most obvious emotion driving this behavior is pride. Members felt a strong sense of pride at sharing their own progress.

Young understood her members well enough to know pride could be a powerful driver of goal-setting and tracking. She wanted members to realize how far they had come to achieving their goals. Her first strategy would be to make her members feel proud.

But if the strategy was designed to help members feel proud of their progress, what happens to the members who don't progress? What happens to those who fall off the wagon, stop exercising, or give up on their treatment plan? What happens to the people who *most need the support of others?* Are they left behind to be ignored? Young knew she needed this unique group of members to feel accepted and try again:

> *"We work really hard at making [Mayo Connect] a place where you can also fail. It's ok to say you started smoking again because we'll be there for you the next time you try [to quit]. We give people the confidence not only to succeed but also the peers to support them when they fail".*

Not all strategies need to harness positive emotions. Negative emotions also are valid for strategy. Alleviating a sense of frustration, fear, and loneliness is as indispensable as making members feel pride, joy, and a sense of belonging. Amplifying negative emotions might even be more powerful than amplifying positive emotions. No one rushes to the store to buy vitamins. Emotions like jealousy or fear of losing social standing can drive people to make extraordinary contributions to any community.

Young had her first two strategies, making members feel proud and accepted, but she also needed strategies to get members answering their questions and sharing their expertise. Young spoke to members to get a sense of their motivations. Two opposing challenges stood out. Members who had been helped by Mayo Clinic truly wanted to give back and help others who had been in the same situation. They felt joy in helping others (and possibly guilt if they didn't). But these same members didn't often feel they had enough knowledge and expertise to help one another. They didn't feel *confident* in being able to help other people. The strategies almost revealed themselves.

Young would make members feel a sense of pride in their progress, acceptance if they fail, joy in giving back, and confidence in having useful expertise to share. Each strategy targeted a different segment of members. Now the entire effort, shown below, began to crystallize into a single sheet.

Goal(s)	IMPROVE THE HEALTH AND WELLBEING OF MEMBERS			
Objectives	Get *new members* to set goals and share progress		Get *top members* (those who have been through treatment) to answer questions and share their experiences	
Strategies	Make members feel a sense of pride in achieving their goals and showing progress	Make members feel accepted to come back to the community even if they fail	Make members feel joy in giving back	Make members feel confident they have useful expertise to share

Young's next challenge was to find the best tactics to make members feel these emotions. A tactic isn't designed to get members to do something, but to make members *feel* something. It's these feelings, these emotions, which are the fuel for member behaviors. A community which provokes the right emotions is the one which gets members to make the right kind of contributions.

Tactics

No shortage of potentially terrific tactics to engage members are available, from jokes to live interviews with celebrities. But true success comes from selecting the right tactics and committing to them. These are the tactics that have the biggest possible impact and best help members *feel* the emotion that drives the right actions.

Almost every brand community manager is trying to do too many things with too little time. Many are trying to deploy over twenty tactics a week. When one tactic isn't working, they add another, and another, and another. They divide precious time into smaller chunks while hoping for bigger results.

Gordon Ramsay, a celebrity chef, built a reputation as a troubleshooter on his TV show *Kitchen Nightmares*. In almost every episode, he cuts the number of items on the menu from dozens, sometimes hundreds, to just a handful. Most chefs hate the constraints, but it works. It helps the restaurant build a reputation around a particular type of food and focuses the chef on becoming good in a few meals. This keeps customers coming back.

FeverBee's work with clients is often similar. FeverBee cuts the number of tactics clients are executing from dozens to just a few (usually five to seven). Like the chefs in *Kitchen Nightmares*, some don't respond well at first. But the results speak for themselves. It's always more effective to do a small number of things extraordinarily well than many things badly. The challenge is knowing what to to do (and, just as importantly, what not to do).

Young's tactics are subtle but significant. For example, she's made over 4,000 posts in the community. A typical post reads:

"Posted by @colleenyoung, Sun, Apr 8 8:04pm."

@aarniek, thanks for starting this discussion specifically about spasticity. I'd like to invite @hopeful33250 @hump1278 @maryar and @magg to also join the discussion.

Have you tried physio? Is splinting, bracing or casting an option for you?

This post doesn't seem especially strategic, probably no different from millions of other posts on the web. But a deeper look shows Young is amplifying the emotions she wants members to feel. By introducing members to one another, she's helping members feel accepted (strategy 2). By asking a follow-up question, she's helping them feel confident (strategy 3); by tagging in other people, she's making them feel confident they have knowledge to share (strategy 3) and giving them the opportunity to experience joy in helping others (strategy 4).

Young isn't randomly responding to feel busy; she's deliberately executing her strategy. Each one of the 4,000 posts is part of her strategy to get her members to feel the things she needs them to feel. Her posts are just one of the core tactics she's using today.

Young also set up badges and levels to appear on their profiles as members hit each target. This visible progress helps foster a strong sense of pride. Members can visibly see their progress. It's a simple, but effective, win for everyone.

Next, Young wanted members to feel confidence and joy in sharing their knowledge and expertise. She created the *Mayo Connect Mentor* program. Each mentor is invited to tell their story and reach out to people who are struggling.[113] This program provided members not only with a sense of exclusivity but also made it easy for members to feel joy in helping other members.

But making it *easy* for members to share their story is only one side of the challenge; the other was to make them feel confident enough to do this. For this, Young reached for a common tool for community builders. She helped them find their superpower.

A popular concept in community building is known as Asset-based Community Development (ABCD).[114] Instead of looking at a community through the prism of a problem to be solved (e.g. crime), ABCD looks for what attributes members can contribute for the benefit of the group (i.e. members are treated as assets). Every member has something they can contribute (time, skills, knowledge, resources), Young's work was to help members identify their superpower.

"We have a mentor who is a former journalist. He's our researcher. Someone else, who works in customer support, is often the person we call upon when someone is having technical difficulties. Another mentor is particularly insightful and empathetic with people facing mental health issues. All

---

113   https://connect.mayoclinic.org/champions/why-become-a-champion/
       https://connect.mayoclinic.org/page/about-connect/tab/
       volunteer-mentors/

114   Kretzmann, J., McKnight, J. (1993). *Building Communities From the Inside Out: A Path Toward Finding and Mobilizing a Community's Assets* (3rd ed.). Chicago, IL: ACTA Publications.

have different assets, not necessarily the reason that brought them to Connect, and now it's a badge of honour."

When people identify their superpower, their confidence goes up. The more confident members feel, the more likely they are to help others and share their own stories and expertise. Here's the complete strategic plan:

Goal(s)	IMPROVE THE HEALTH AND WELLBEING OF MEMBERS			
Objectives	Get *new members* to set goals and share progress		Get *top members* (those who have been through treatment) to answer questions and share their experiences	
Strategies	Make members feel a sense of pride in achieving their goals and showing progress.	Make members feel accepted to come back to the community even if they fail.	Make members feel joy in giving back.	Make members feel confident they have useful expertise to share.
Tactics	Use gamification tools (badges and levels) for members to set targets and report progress.	Direct responses in messages and communications to build a sense of belonging (and confidence).	Build a Mentor program for people to step forward and commit to giving something back.	Get each member to identify their superpower and show how they can contribute it to the group.

Young's tactics are simple and effective. They all take place at the micro-level, the very level most brands take for granted. The best strategies in the world fail without someone like Young doing the hard work of forging a community at the most minute levels. Every post and update brings the community close to achieving its goals.

Summary

The success of every brand community hinges upon how well a community manager can operate at the one-to-one level. After the investments have been made, the grand vision set, and the community launched to the masses, it all boils down to *how well can a brand community manager execute? Can they make members feel something that matters?*

Technology can help, but skills make the real difference. The more skilled the people running the community, the more successful it will be. Perhaps the great mistake for brand communities in the past decade has been a whopping over-investment in technology and underinvestment in the people to manage the community.

A junior salesperson would never be given the keys to a Ferrari and told to manage sales for a brand's best customers. But interns and low-level staff are often told to manage technology, which costs more than a Ferrari and is filled with the brand's best customers. They can come up with a lot of great tactics, but few seem to make members feel the emotion they need to feel. That's because they're the wrong tactics in the first place. The end result is an overwhelmed community manager trying as many tactics as possible and hoping something works.

In another pair of hands, Mayo Clinic Connect remains a ghost town filled with Mayflies. It never becomes indispensable. No technology in the world can make people feel the things a community manager can make them feel.

The subtle, yet critical, work Young does each day is all part of a strategy. It ties back to improving how her members feel emotionally and, eventually, becomes a huge benefit for her colleagues. The impact the community has on its users and her colleagues becomes more obvious with each passing day. Young notes she doesn't "*have enough hours of the day to answer all the requests and meet with all the different departments and clinicians who want to get involved with the community now.*"

Young has turned Mayo Connect from a platform filled with Mayfly carcasses into a buzzing, indispensable, community for the organization and members alike. It's a place where members are constantly sharing their own amazing stories:

> "*When people post their stories of success, like wearing a smaller pant size because of the support of the community, or getting through cancer treatment with less anxiety, it's incredible.*"

Throughout the entire time, she was a realist, not a purist; she knew the community needed to deliver results. Young didn't write a dust-collecting 50+ page strategy. She kept it simple. She didn't avoid her colleagues, she sought them out. She uncovered what her colleagues most cared about and ensured the community was designed to have a big impact.

Young didn't just accept a need for engagement, she pushed back and challenged her members to make their most valuable contributions. These contributions lifted the value of the entire community. She didn't take the easy path. She didn't ask members to connect, like, and share. She asked them to set targets, come back if they fell short of them, and become mentors who share their own stories to help others. She focused on raising the bar of engagement, not lowering it.

Young managed to thread the needle between what her organization needed and what members wanted. Then she lit an emotional fire under her members to get results, results her colleagues cared about. She was smart about which tactics she selected but, once selected, she committed everything to achieving them. Young's strategy achieved precisely what a strategy should achieve: it made her community indispensable.

CONCLUSION

In November 2017, six months after our first interview, Maria Ogneva is again sitting in LinkedIn's canteen, talking about her final community project at LinkedIn. She still loves and believes in community, but the same realisation that drove her to become an indispensable community professional also revealed the limits of being *just* a community professional:

> *"I feel like I'm coming to the end of my community career. I've gone about as high as I can go and learnt about as much as I can."*

Community professionals peak low in the organizational chart. There just aren't enough "*chief of community*" roles in the world, even in community-driven organizations like LinkedIn.[115] Being '*the community person*' is great for a job, bad for a profession. To keep climbing, Maria feels she needs to decide which business function she's ultimately working within. Is she in customer support, customer success, human resources, marketing, product or something else? It's a difficult decision.

Building an indispensable community (or, in Ogneva's case, several indispensable communities) is one of the most valuable things anyone can do in any organization. An indispensable community is an asset that long outlives its creator. It delivers tremendous value for colleagues. It changes how members feel about the organization. It can serve as a career accelerator and lift professionals straight to the top of the community profession. But, alas, the community profession only goes so high.

In the future, more organizations may have senior community staff reporting to the CEO where people like Ogneva can thrive.

---

115 There are some, but these are largely in large tech companies clustered on the west coast of the USA.

It would be great to conclude by saying these roles exist today, *go get them...the future is yours!* This book, however, is about being a realist and seeing the world as it is.[116] If we want these roles, we need to work hard to create them ourselves.

We need to wake up each morning with a belief and passion for what a brand community can be and take a tiny step forward each day to make that a reality. We need to resist pressure from colleagues, avoid the engagement trap, and help members to make even better contributions today than they did yesterday. We need to take yet another meeting with yet another colleague, listen to yet more concerns, and overcome their resistance with each tiny victory.

It's going to be tempting to give up on the vision for what the community can be and give in to the pressure for engagement today. There will be times when we will lose hope in members when things don't progress the right way. Push back against that. The countless stories in this book have shown it is possible to build a better community.

When we commit to driving better results from the community and motivating better contributions from members to the community, the foundations for an indispensable community will begin to take shape. That indispensable community is something you, your members, and your organization can take great pride and joy in. It's a powerful flywheel, and, as the community starts to show results, it gets more resources which can deliver better results.

If we commit our own time, talent, and motivation to following the advice shared by dozens of community professionals in this book, we will get there. Nothing is more exciting, rewarding, and fulfilling than building a community your colleagues and your members find *indispensable.*

Acknowledgements

When I began this book in late 2016, I had no idea I'd be still writing it in June 2018. I had no idea how much travel it would

---

116 Two months after the interview, Maria left LinkedIn to become Director of Customer Experience at FinancialForce.

take, the number of rewrites, the late nights spent working on the balcony alone, and the social cost. My wife, Skirmante, has always supported me and deserves all the gratitude I can give her.

A huge thank you to my editor, Robin Dellabough, whose feedback was often infuriating to hear, but always correct and astute. Robin made this an infinitely better book and once again proved herself indispensable.

I remember a game designer telling me once, at the Game Developer Conference, *"the really hard part is when you're 75% of the way through and you lose all objective understanding of whether what you're creating is any good."* This is where my allies in the FeverBee community stepped in and provided amazing feedback that led me to rewrite whole sections, clarify key points, and cut entire chapters. In no particular order, a huge thank you to: Adrian Speyer, Rebecca Braglio, Piper Wilson, Samantha Preddie, Neofytos Kolokotronis, Yannis Triantafyllou, Wouter Schrijvershof, Xhevair Maskuli, Nick Emmett, Marjorie Anderson, Luke Zimmer, Kristen Gestaldo, Kathleen Ulrich, Jessica Malnik, Janice James, Emily Dunn, Ernesto Izquierdo, Dave Sciuto, Corinna Snyder, Melissa Jenkins, Ale Fattorini, Joe DeLisle, Lillian Bejtlich, Katelyn MacKenzie, Lora Dimitrova, and Carson Weitnauer.

I'm equally grateful to my current and former colleagues at FeverBee. One of the biggest sacrifices in writing this book has been the inability to support the team the way I would have wanted and I'm eternally grateful for their understanding and enduring professionalism. A huge thanks to Darren Gough, Sarah Hawk, Todd Nilson, Phil Betts, Nancy Kinder.

And a truly special thanks to Clare Layton, my virtual assistant, who has arranged almost every trip (the one time I booked my own flight I forgot about it and booked it twice), scheduled every meeting and phone call this book required.

I'm in complete debt to the incredible community professionals who put their trust in me and were willing to share their stories on the record. Many shared not only their successes but their failures and challenges, too. Others helped supply facts and information off the record. A few pestered their CEOs to find time to speak to me, too. I hope to have repaid their trust by narrating them faithfully. I'm also immensely grateful to the people who went through countless legal channels to be *allowed* to share their stories, their metrics, and walk me through how their community teams function.

A special thanks to Allison Leahy, Colleen Young, and Maria Ogneva, three of the most incredible community professionals on the planet, who deserve all the recognition and rewards they will certainly duly receive.

A further huge thank you to Simona Ciampi, Eduardo Giansante, Ruben Martin, Jay Gordon, Lois Townsend, Allison Brotman, Amanda Graham, Ben Munoz, Matthew Cox, Elio Garcia, Rex Williams, Michelle Aggiato, Dayna Britton, Alicia Nakamoto, Evan Hamilton, Timo Tolonen, Ceri Hughes, Gordon Strause, Andy Sernovitz, Tony Woodall, Gali Kling Schneider, Brenton Murray, Barbara Konchinski, Mark Organ, Grant Packard, Paul Elsey, Dianne Kibbey, Peter Friedman, Matt Roney, Rob Ludlow, Diana Wong, Jacqueline Pike, Bill Johnston, Duncan Field, Ivory Harey, James Pickstone, Chris Savage, Margot Mazur, Joe Cothrel, Jeremy Demers, Zach Taylor, Tony Woodall, Suzi Nelson, Kevin Goddard, Michael Wu, Jess Spate, Rosemary Tietge, Lee Aase, Stephanie Norris, Tricia Lawrence, Jennifer Cohan, Madison Carey, Ivan Butina, Gemma Howells, Lance Rougeux, David Tchozewski, Charlie Hoehn, Anna Soellner, Christina Griffin, Jaime Anstee, Sam Houston, Bliss Hanlon, Phoebe Vankat, Jennifer Lopez, Nathan Maton, Lana Lee, Philippe Beaudette, Eric Shaw, Ryan Paredez, and many others who provided background information but wished to remain off the record.

A huge thank you also to Rachel Happe, Jim Storer, David Spinks, Vanessa Dimauro, and many others who work hard every day to drive the building of communities forward. I'm proud to be in an indispensable community with each of you.

About Richard Millington

Richard Millington is the founder of FeverBee, a consultancy and community, which has helped 250+ organizations (including Apple, Facebook, Google, SAP, Wikipedia, The World Bank, Greenpeace etc) build indispensable communities. Over the past 13 years, FeverBee's work has collectively shaped the behavior of 500m+ community members from around the world.

Richard is also the author of *Buzzing Communities: How to Build Bigger, Better, And More Active Online Communities (2011)* and the creator of five courses in successful community management. FeverBee's courses have trained 1200+ community professionals to understand and deliver what their members and colleagues truly need. Graduates include community professionals at Reddit, Google, Fitbit, Amazon, Lego, Spotify, and many more.

Richard has spoken at hundreds of events across 25 countries and has been featured in *The Guardian, The Economist, Al Jazeera,* and elsewhere.

You can find out more about Richard and FeverBee at www.FeverBee.com.

INDEX

B

backlash, 26, 64, 140
badges, 42, 89, 160–61
battle, 16, 19, 62, 146, 148,
  152
  big, 20
beliefs, 156, 166
  purist community, 99
benefits, 13, 18, 51, 53, 64–66,
  71–72, 74, 77, 79, 87, 117,
  122, 124–25, 136, 150
  important, 66
  supposed, 104
BestBuy, 40
bloggers, 57–58
  active, 85
  fellow, 56
  hired chief, 57
blog posts, 13, 17, 75
  short, 62
boss, 13, 96–97, 99, 151
  community manager's, 151
brand ambassadors, 131
brand communities, ix–xi, 9,
  11, 39–40, 102–5, 117–19,
  126–27, 130, 133, 135,
  137–39, 146–47, 152,
  161–62, 166
brand managers, vii
brand position, official, 142
brands, vii, ix–xii, 10–11,
  15–18, 24, 40–41, 46–48,
  64–66, 68–69, 80–81,
  101–2, 104, 131, 153–54,
  161–62
  popular, 101
browsing, 13, 135

guests, 39
budget, 13, 31, 90, 117, 131,
  137, 142, 148
  annual, 24
  limited, 76, 89
building, ix–x, xii, 71, 73,
  98–99, 102–3, 105, 107,
  114, 124, 126, 136–37,
  144–45, 148, 165–66
business, viii, xi–xii, 34, 41,
  49, 53–54, 56–57, 95–96,
  98–99, 109–10, 119, 135,
  146, 149
Business Insider, 142
business metrics, 58
business software, 14

C

Canadian Cancer Society, 148
Canadian Virtual Hospice,
  148
care, 56, 63–64, 66, 70, 120,
  123–24, 134, 149
  advertisers, 109
  patient, 150
  product customers, 81
  senior leaders, 133–34
CEO, 17, 19, 53, 104, 112,
  119–20, 133, 143, 151, 165,
  168
  company's, 132
  game's, 20
  new, 26, 131
CFO, 104, 142, 151
  new, 110
challenges, 60–61, 109, 128,
  150–51, 157, 167

CPSIA information can be obtained
at www.ICGtesting.com
Printed in the USA
FSHW01n0817190918